MARIO BIGON AND
GUIDO REGAZZONI

THE
CENTURY
GUIDE
TO KNOTS

647 photographs in colour

FOR SAILING

FISHING

CAMPING

CLIMBING

Translated from the Italian
by Maria Piotrowska

D0582779

CENTURY
London Sydney Auckland Johannesburg

Translated from the Italian by Maria Piotrowska

Originally published in Italian in Italy in 1981 by
Arnoldo Mondadori Editore under the title "Guida ai Nodi"

First publi hed in Great Britain in 1983

This paperback edition first published in 1988 by
Century Hutchinson Ltd
Brookmount House, 62-65 Chandos Place,
Covent Garden, London WC2N 4NW

Century Hutchinson Australia Pty Ltd
20 Alfred Street, Milsons Point,
Sydney, NSW 2061, Australia

Century Hutchinson New Zealand Ltd
P.O.Box 40-086, Glenfield,
Auckland 10, New Zealand

Century Hutchinson South Africa Pty Ltd
P.O.Box 337, Bergvlei, 2012 South Africa

Reprinted 1989

ISBN: 0 7126 2304 3

Printed and bound by
Officine Grafiche di Arnoldo Mondadori Editore,
Verona, Italy

THE
CENTURY
GUIDE
TO KNOTS

CONTENTS

9 Cordage

25 **Utility knots**
27 Stopper knots
39 Hitches
67 Loops
99 Running knots
107 Shortenings
115 Tackle
119 Bends

143 **Knots for fishermen**

181 **Decorative and applied knots**
183 Decorative knots
235 Applied knots

247 Glossary
250 Knots and their uses
252 Bibliography
253 Index

The aim of this handbook is basically instructive, so we have concentrated on two specific aspects: illustrations and terminology. We consider illustrations to be the simplest and most immediate way of explaining how a knot is tied, so we have filmed every step and arranged the photographs in a logical sequence, showing each stage from the viewpoint of the person tying the knot. You need only take a length of rope and follow the photographs step by step to find that you have the completed knot in your hand.

The terminology used has been subordinated to the illustrations and, with the exception of a few concessions to the art of seamanship, has been kept as simple as possible. All you need remember is that *working* means tightening and shaping and that a *turn* is one round of a rope to be able to understand the book fully. For the terms *end* and *standing part*, refer to the illustrations. The *end* (2) is the termination of the rope or the free part towards the termination of the rope with which the knot is tied; the *standing part* (1) is the part which is not actively used in making the knot and around which the knot is tied by the end. The slack part of the rope between the end and the standing part is the *bight*, especially when it forms a loop or a semicircle as at point 3 of the illustration.

One final word: it is not necessary to know a great number of knots; four or five—such as the bowline, the sheet bend, the clove hitch, and the figure-eight knot—are sufficient to cope confidently with any situation. The most important thing is to know how to tie them quickly and properly and with the minimum number of movements. The only way to gain the necessary confidence is to practice the knots over and over again until the movements become completely automatic and instinctive, for in certain circumstances hesitation or doubt can make the knot an enemy or at least a dangerous complication instead of a safety factor.

1. standing part   2. end   3. bight

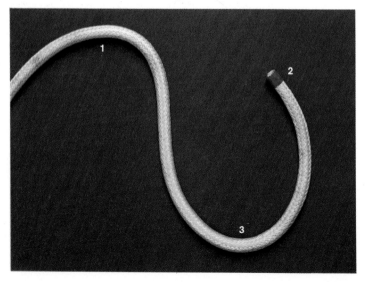

cordage

cordage

Rope was one of man's first inventions, certainly predating the wheel, and its structure has remained essentially the same for centuries, although the advent of synthetic fibers has given it a strength comparable, and in certain ways superior, to that of steel.

Rope and *knot* are two words that go hand in hand, for one is useless without the other; what use is a length of rope without at least one knot in it? Up to a few decades ago, the choice of rope was limited: hemp and manilla were used for their strength, cotton for manageability, and sisal for economy; but today the availability of synthetic fibers has produced a specialized type of rope for every application.

structure

Rope is made up of fibers (a) twisted together a number of times, each in the opposite direction to the previous one, to form, first of all, the yarn (b), then the strands (c) and finally the rope itself. This operation is known as laying up and produces the classic rope generally made up of three (1) and sometimes more strands (2), but there is another way of producing rope, namely by braiding the yarn (3) instead of twisting it together; with this kind of rope the outer part, known as the sheath (e), is both a protective and an attractive

covering, while the strength of the rope lies solely in its internal part which is also braided and is known as the core (d). Both types of rope have their own special characteristics which make them better suited to certain applications; twisted rope is less flexible and better for heavy-duty work, whereas braided rope is a lot softer and if pre-stretched does not expand any further. Rope should be bought with a view to choosing the most suitable type for the job you have in mind.

materials

The characteristics of a rope obviously depend to a great extent on the fibers that make it up, so it is useful to know what the characteristics of the different materials are. From this you can deduce those of the corresponding rope.

The names of the materials may be somewhat confused as chemical names like polyester are freely mixed with the manufacturer's brand names such as Tergal, Dacron, etc. The following list gives only the chemical classifications and the table on page 14 gives the most common brand names for the equivalent products. It should also be noted that manufacturing companies now offer many variants of the same product (with greater or less strength, elasticity etc.). The following data refer to average characteristics.

a. fiber   b. yarn   c. strand   d. core   e. sheath
1 and 2. twisted rope   3. braided rope

Natural fibers

Natural fibers have now almost completely been replaced by synthetics, but the most commonly used were hemp, manilla, cotton, and sisal. It is still possible to come across rope made of hemp, which up to a few years ago was the best material available for rope. The advantages of this material are its tensile strength and an excellent resistance to wear and atmospheric agents, which is even better than that of synthetic fibers. Its disadvantages are that it is heavy (especially when wet) and is not very elastic, but particularly that it rots easily and has to be stored carefully.

Synthetic fibers

As their name suggests, these fibers are compounded by man from oil or coal derivatives. They are all shiny, non-absorbent, do not rot, and have low melting points. The production processes involved make it possible to improve features such as the fineness, strength, and elasticity. In general, an increase in the strength of a rope corresponds with a decrease in its flexibility. Greater fineness is associated with greater strength and flexibility but also with less abrasion resistance. The most common fibers are polypropylene, polyamide, and polyester, but to complete the picture, we have also included polyethylene and aramid.

Polypropylene fibers
(commonly known as olefin)

These are widely used in commercial sailing, as they combine low cost with excellent mechanical qualities and abrasion resistance. They also have very high resistance to atmospheric agents, light, and the hydrocarbons that are always present on the surfaces of commercial ports. This is the only fiber that floats well, so it is most suitable for use in water skiing tow ropes, rescue lines, and for mooring large ships. It is not commonly used in competitive sailing, possibly because it is cheaper than other types of rope.

Polyamide fibers
(commonly known as nylon)

These fibers offer excellent characteristics for rope, as they combine strength and elasticity, enabling them to absorb shock loads better than any other material. They do not rot or float. The fibers can be modified chemically to produce other products which vary slightly from one another (nylon 6, nylon 66, and nylon 11) and are used in climbing rope. Fishing line is also made of polyamide fibers, as it has to be both tough and flexible and must allow knots to be made in it and to hold well.

Polyester fibers

Polyester fibers have the best mechanical qualities combined with low elasticity and so are a good choice for rope to be used in sailing. They are highly resistant to wear and atmospheric agents and can be pre-stretched to reduce deformation under strain. They do not float.

Polyethylene fibers

Ropes made of polyethylene fibers should be avoided. They are very cheap, but they are not very strong, and they stretch and slip easily, so they do not hold a knot well. Added to this is the fact that they are difficult to handle. They are, however, very resistant to atmospheric agents and also float. They are used for lifelines on rowboats and rafts, as tow ropes for water skiing, and as rescue lines.

Aramid fibers

These are the newest of the synthetic fibers used for ropes. They are manufactured by Dupont under the name Kevlar. The product has characteristics which are more comparable to those of steel than to the common synthetic fibers. In fact, this material does not melt, but decomposes at about 500°C (932°F) and has a breaking strain equal to that of steel of the same section, although it is slightly more elastic. It is not very resistant to light and does not float. It is used to a limited extent in halyards and sheets for racing boats which need ever lighter materials which do not deform. A rope made of this material is four times stronger than steel of the same weight, but the use of aramid rope is still limited because of its very high cost.

Commercial names of the main synthetic fibers

Polypropylene (olefin)	Meraklon
Polyamide (nylon)	Perlon, Lilion, Enkalon
Polyester	Dacron, Terylene, Tergal, Terital, Trevira, Diolen, Wistel
Aramid	Kevlar, Arenka

Comparison between fibers used in ropemaking

	Hemp	Polyethylene	Polypropylene	Polyamide	Polyester	Aramid
Specific gravity	1.48	0.95	0.91	1.14	1.38	1.44
Melting point	—	135°C	175°C	255°C	260°C	—
Breaking strain (gr/m²)	900	376	455	900	1250	2600
Toughness	5÷7.5	3÷5	4÷6	6÷8	7.5÷8.5	18
Stretching or break %	1.5÷4	15÷35	20/30	19	14	3.7
Moisture regain %	12	0	0.4	4.5	0.5	6

How to choose a rope

The choice of rope should be based on what it will ultimately be used for and should also take into consideration both the material it is made of and the type (braided or twisted).

Choosing on the basis of material

	Anchorage	Mooring	Towing	Rigging and stays	Halyards
Polypropylene		X	X		
Polyamide	X	X	X		
Polyester	X	X		X	X
Aramid				X	X

Choice based on the lay

Twisted rope	Braided rope
More rigid	Softer and easier to handle; slides more easily through snap-links and fairleads
Keeps its circular section	Flattens and holds better on winch drums
Excellent resistance to wear, loses resistance gradually as wear increases	Does not lose its resistance until the core is damaged
All parts of the rope are clearly visible so it has no secrets	May have hidden flaws beneath the sheath, or, more often, *cheating*, particularly the use of cheaper types of fiber
Grips the knot very well	Some knots come undone too easily
Can be spliced to steel cable	Using core with very little elasticity, you can have rope that does not stretch (excellent for halyards)
Basically a rope for heavy duty work (anchoring, mooring, etc.)	More versatile rope, more manageable and often more attractive

Maintenance

Because of its structure, rope is quite a sturdy product and does not need any special attention. It is important to keep it dry to avoid the formation of mildew and to clean off thoroughly any grease or tar deposits. The only danger is heat which can cause irreparable damage, especially to synthetic fibers with low melting points. So ropes must be kept away from direct heat sources and should not be used on small-diameter pulleys (less than 5 or 6 times the diameter of the rope under tension). Heat generated by friction can cause damage similar to fire. Another point to watch out for is the fraying of the ends due to the slipperiness of the fibers: if the end is not backspliced properly, it will soon fray, eating up yards and yards of rope.

Rope used in sailing should be washed at the end of the season with a standard detergent for delicate clothing. Drying is very important, and care should be taken to dry the rope right through. Any tar or oil stains can be bleached away with careful use of gasoline or trichloroethylene.

Useful points to remember

- A knot uniting two ropes reduces the strength of the unit to about half that of the weaker rope.

- A rope that is twice the diameter of another has four times its strength.

- Never use two ropes of different materials together, as only the more rigid rope will work under the strain.

- It is not always true that a stronger rope is better, as elasticity also has to be taken into consideration, and if the rope has to take shock loads, polyester polyamides are the best.

- Do not use ropes that float for anchorage in ports, as they would immediately be severed by the propellors of motor boats.

- Use floating lines only for rescue work, light buoys, etc.

- Repair fraying ends immediately; apart from looking untidy, they quickly consume yards and yards of rope.

- Always dry a rope before coiling it down: a rinse with fresh water removes any absorbent salt deposits.

- Do not buy rope which is too stiff and do not believe any salesman who tells you that it will get more supple with time. Similarly, do not trust twisted rope which is too soft, as it can give you a very unpleasant surprise the first time you use it.

COILING DOWN A CABLE

Knowing how to coil down a cable properly is important in order to avoid its becoming a mass of knots and tangles, which would make the rope useless when needed.

How to coil the cable
First of all, follow the direction of the lay of the rope (1). Form the turns of the coil using the wrist (2), laying them in a clockwise direction and taking care to keep them all the same length (3).

1

USING A CLEAT

Wind the halyard onto the cleat using the sailor's method; then coil up the end running free (1). Put your left hand through the coil and take hold of the halyard as close as you can to the cleat (2). Twist it slightly to make a small loop; pull it towards you; pass it over the coil; then slip it over the cleat (3). Check that everything is good and tight, so that the coil will not come loose with the rolling of the boat.

HANGING A CABLE

When a cable has been coiled, it should be tied off so that it can be hung tidily to take up less room. Hanging the rope also helps it to last longer and means it can be used immediately when it is needed.

Method
Coil the rope (see page 18), leaving an end of a yard or more and make a good long bight (1). Wind this bight once clockwise around the top of the coil (2), pass it under its own standing part and pull taut (3). Continuing in a clockwise direction, repeat the same operation (4, 5). Photograph 6 shows the final result: the two turns are tightly drawn up, and the coil can be hung up tidily. Make sure that none of the turns comes away from the coil when you are securing it. If they do, it is better to start again from scratch.

3

5

4

6

STORING
A ROPE

2

1

3

Before putting a rope away, there are a few basic things to be done to keep it in good condition for a long time. First of all, check that the ends are not frayed. If they are, they should be cut and fused again to bind them; then uncoil the rope in the direction of the lay and seize the ends. Clean away any tar stains, and if it is twisted or kinked run it counterclockwise through a block and lay it on the ground in large turns to allow the strands to settle.

Method
Coil the rope (see page 18), leaving an end long enough for the following operations: make three or four turns around the coil (1, 2); fold a bight and insert it into the top of the coil (3); open the bight and bend it back over the top of the coil (4); tighten it by pulling the end (5). When drawing the hitch taut, check that the turns are even; the rope should never be tightened unevenly.

5

utility knots

stopper knots

As their name suggests, stoppers are knots made in the end of a rope to prevent its slipping through an eye or other aperture when the rope is being used. They are also used to bind the strands of a rope.

Stopper knots are used at sea at the ends of the running rigging and to weight heaving lines, as well as in climbing, camping, and fishing. These knots can also be used decoratively, though in this case they may be made in the central part of the rope as well as at the end.

The most important knots of this type are the overhand knot, which is as old as man himself and is used as the basis for countless other knots; the figure-eight knot, which is the stopper most used by sailors and also the lovers' knot in heraldry; and the heaving line and multiple overhand knots, which are used to weight the ends of ropes and as decorative knots.

◀ 1. Overhand knot   2. Multiple overhand knot
3. Figure-eight knot   4. Heaving line knot.

OVERHAND KNOT

As generally used, the word knot has several meanings and can indicate anything from a fastening to a tangle of rope or other flexible material. Of course accidental knots and tangles have not been included in this book. Splices, too, are beyond its scope. The knot also has a religious significance: in ancient times it was considered a pact, a

1

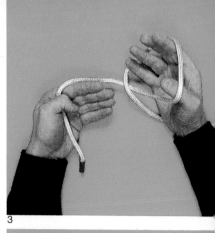

2

3

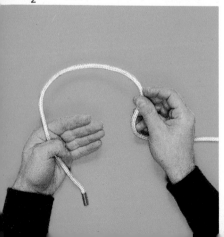

4

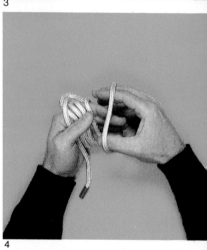

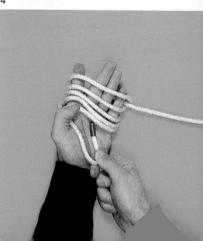

bond, a symbol with magic powers.

The overhand knot is used in many situations: It is used as a basis for other knots, to hold objects when the tension on both ends is equal, as a terminal or stopper knot, and, finally, it is tied at regular intervals along lifelines. An obvious but very useful application of this knot is at the end of sewing thread passed through the eye of a needle. It is not popular with sailors, as it is impossible to untie when wet if it has been tied tightly.

Method
Turn the standing part to make a loop and pass the end through it (1).

How to make a series of overhand knots
The left hand holds the end and the turns formed by the right hand (2, 3). To form these turns close your right hand and use the thumb to hook up the standing part by twisting your wrist from the bottom upwards so that the rope winds around the fingers (2, 3). Slip the turns onto the left hand as soon as they are formed, keeping them regular and in order without letting them overlap (4). Now pass the end through the turns from left to right (5, 6) and continue pulling the end in the same direction to form, as if by magic, as many knots as there are turns, spaced at regular intervals (7, 8).

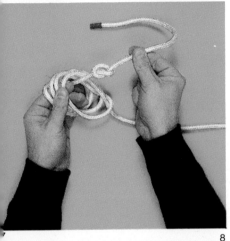

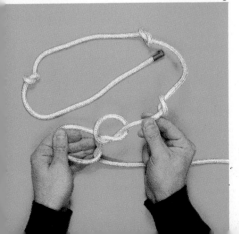

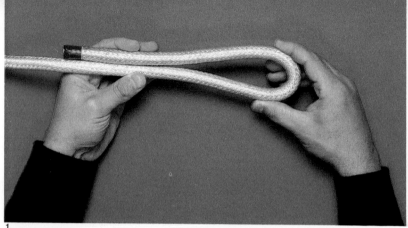

FIGURE-EIGHT KNOT

First method

This knot is known in Italy as the Savoy knot because it appears in the coat of arms of the House of Savoy. In heraldry it is known as the love knot for it symbolizes faithful love and eternal friendship, but it is most widely known as the figure-eight knot because of its characteristic shape. It is made in the end of a rope with the upper loop nipping the standing part and the lower loop nipping the end.

The figure-eight knot is the most important stopper knot used by sailors. It is used on the running rigging whenever the lines do not end in wall knots.

Method
Make a bight near the end of a rope without twisting it in any way (1). Holding the rope securely with the left hand, take the tip of the bight in the right hand and make two half twists turning the wrist upwards (1, 2). Then pass the end through the eye of the bight to produce immediately a figure-eight-shaped knot (3, 4). If this does not occur it is because the twists are not correct. The knot is drawn taut by pulling both ends at the same time.

31

FIGURE-EIGHT KNOT

Second method

This method is used when making the knot in large-diameter rope which cannot be held in the hand because of its size and weight.

Method
Begin by making an overhand loop (1); then, passing the end behind the standing part and turning it clockwise, form a second loop, making sure that the shape of the first is not altered (2). Now pass the end into the upper loop and work it by pulling both loose ends at the same time (3).

SLIPPED FIGURE-EIGHT

The loop is useful when you want to hang or add another rope to the knot. In this case, the figure-eight knot must be fairly tight to hold the item hooked.

Method
Allow an end of about half a yard (half a meter), double it, and insert this loop into the upper loop of the knot (4).

FIGURE-EIGHT KNOTS IN SERIES

Making a number of these knots in small stuff can produce delicate chains and necklaces, etc.

Method
Extend the cord on a level surface and form a figure eight (1). To do this make a large loop by twisting the right wrist counterclockwise, then twist the end of the loop clockwise to form the eight. Take care not to twist the standing part along its length. Form as many figure eights as desired at regular intervals (2, 3); then insert the end through the upper loops of those formed, working from right to left (4, 5). Pulling the end through the upper loops along the rope makes the knots (6, 7, 8, 9).

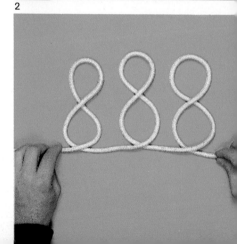

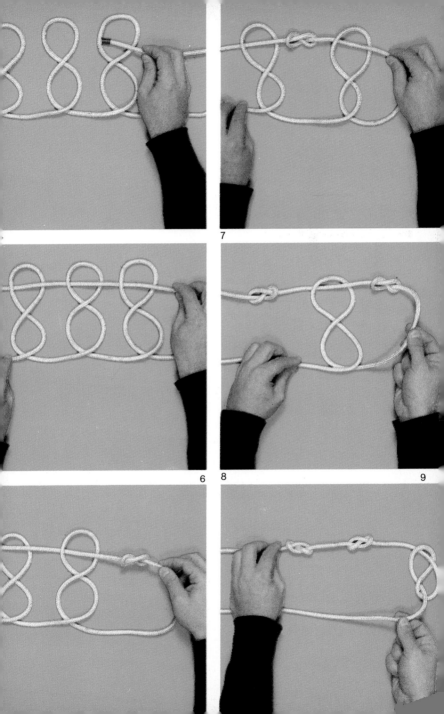

6

7

8

9

HEAVING LINE KNOT

This knot is also known as the Franciscan or monk's knot and is both decorative and practical. The Franciscan friars use it as a weight along the cord they use as a belt. It is also used to weight heaving lines or as a stopper knot on small stuff. The heaving line knot is used by sailors because it is very strong and does not wear the fibers of the rope.

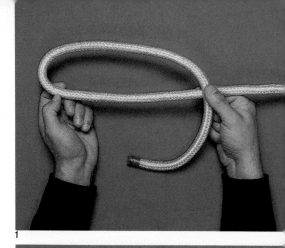

1

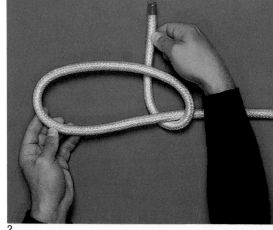

2

Method

Make a long loop at the bight of the cord, leaving the end long enough to form the successive turns. The end must cross the standing part (1). The turns are made regularly from right to left without overlapping each other (2, 3, 4). You can make as many turns as you like; the knot will increase in size the more turns there are. Having done this, pass the end through the loop (5). This is the key to the knot. Finally pull the standing part to tighten the knot (6).

6

MULTIPLE OVERHAND KNOT

The multiple overhand knot is also known as the blood knot because it was tied into the ends of cat-o'-nine-tails. The Capuchin friars make the knot in the length of the cord on their habits to give them weight and make them hang properly. This knot is used by sailors as a weighting or stopper knot on small-diameter line, but it is not highly recommended as it is very difficult to untie, particularly when wet.

Method
Starting with an overhand knot (1), make three or four additional turns with the end, wrapping them snugly. This is very important to the success of the knot (2). Draw the knot up well by pulling both ends with a sharp jerk. This is necessary for the turns to wind tightly together and cover the joint, which thus disappears (3). When the knot is completed only the turns are visible around the cord.

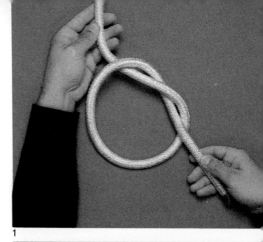

1

2

hitches

Hitches are used for tying a rope to another object. Whenever you have to tie one, it is advisable to have a look at the rope and follow its lay. These knots are often used by sailors for mooring, fastening, and lashing; so they must be able to withstand parallel traction without slipping.

Hitches divide into two categories: crossing knots which include the clove hitch, the cow hitch, and the bill hitch, and knots formed with simple turns, such as the fisherman's bend, the rolling hitch, and the highwayman's hitch.

The illustration on the following pages shows:
1. Cat's-paw   2. Highwayman's hitch   3. Rolling hitch
4. Constrictor knot   5. Fisherman's bend   6. Cow hitch
7. Clove hitch on a ring   8. Half hitches

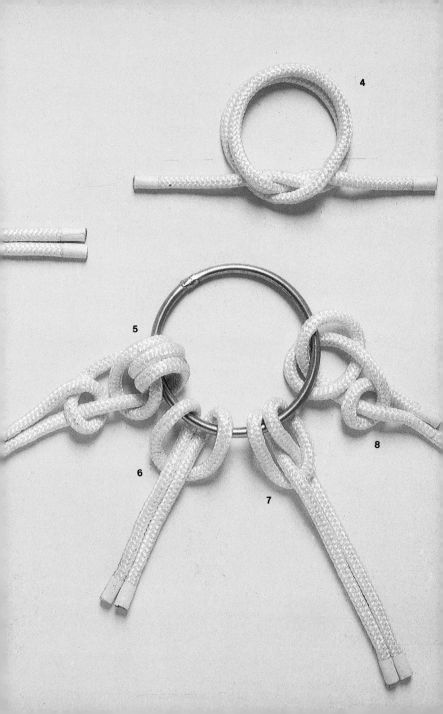

CLOVE HITCH

Tied around a post

The knot known to sailors as the clove hitch is also known under other names such as the peg knot in camping and the boatman's knot in climbing. It is a safe knot which is easy to make and is used in a variety of situations. Sailors use it in small- or medium-diameter rope for mooring; it is used on climbing rope and by campers to secure tent poles.

Method
Make a counterclockwise turn around the post, passing the end in front of it (1). The second turn is made by passing the end back around the post above the first turn without tightening it (2). Then tuck the end through the second turn which should cross over the first (3). Draw the hitch taut by pulling both ends (4).

SLIPPED CLOVE HITCH

The bight serves to undo the knot quickly when the rope is under strain (5).

DOUBLE CLOVE HITCH

To make this knot you need only make an extra turn around the post (6).

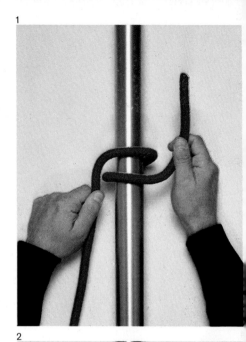

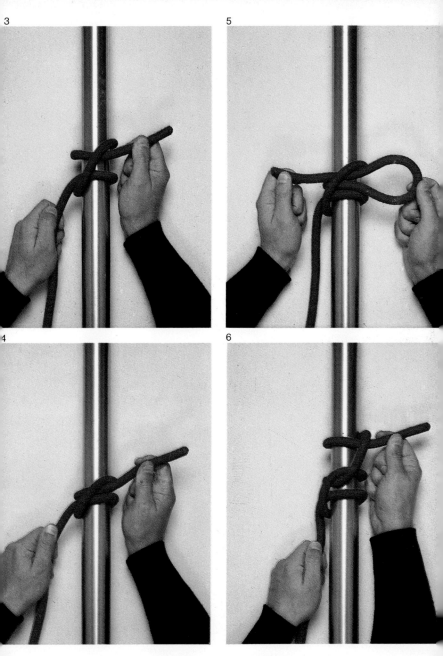

CLOVE HITCH

Made on a ring

The clove hitch on a ring is used almost exclusively on climbing ropes as it can regulate the length of the rope between the climber and the piton. The clove hitch on a ring is rarely used in sailing as the ring is usually finer than the rope so the constant strain on the rope causes chafing. In addition its jamming action is not very secure as it does not have sufficient nip and so could slip and come undone.

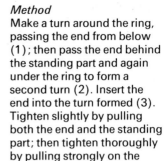

3

Method
Make a turn around the ring, passing the end from below (1); then pass the end behind the standing part and again under the ring to form a second turn (2). Insert the end into the turn formed (3). Tighten slightly by pulling both the end and the standing part; then tighten thoroughly by pulling strongly on the standing part (4).

4

CLOVE HITCH

Using two overlapping half hitches

This method is used in sailing for mooring on bollards at the quayside, or in camping to tighten the guy ropes if the loops can be dropped over the post.

Method
Make a large loop or hitch with the standing part below (1). Hold the loop securely with the left hand and drop it over the post (2). Allowing sufficient length for a second loop, grasp the standing part and twist your wrist upwards and counterclockwise to form a second loop (3, 4); the standing part should now be underneath. Hold the loop thus formed securely with the thumb and forefinger and drop it over the post (5). Pull the two ends of the rope to tighten the knot (6). You should check frequently to be sure the knot is holding and not slipping.

1

2

CLOVE HITCH

Using two inverted loops in a figure eight

This method is very attractive because it is so easy, but it can only be used when the hitch can be dropped over the object.

Method
Form a loop with the end over the standing part (1); hold the loop securely with the left hand. Take the standing part with the right hand, allowing sufficient length for the formation of a second loop and twist the wrist in a clockwise direction (2). The standing part should end up on top. Now flip the bottom loop over the top one (3, 4) and drop them over the post with the right hand, holding the end in the left (5). Tighten the knot by pulling both ends (6).

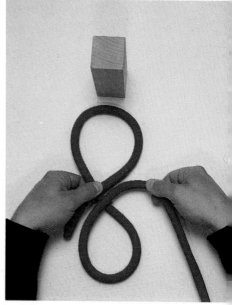

CLOVE HITCH

Using two hands

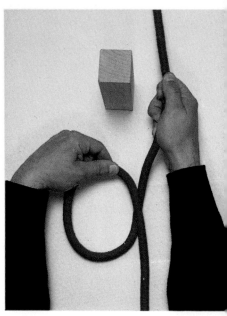

1

4

Normally this method is used when a line has been thrown but only if the rope is not under strain and can be dropped over the object. Sailors use this method when mooring on a bollard at the quayside with medium-diameter rope.

Method
Pick up the rope with the right hand and take hold of it with the left about eighteen inches away. The left palm should be facing downwards (1). Twist the left wrist to form a loop (2). With the right hand, pull the rope towards you and form another loop. The standing part should be lying below the end (3, 4). Overlap the two loops and drop them over the post. Tighten it by pulling the end with your right hand (5).

5

CLOVE HITCH

For a rope under strain

This method is preferred by sailors for mooring a drifting boat.

Method
Take the rope in both hands (1). Jerk the rope with the left hand to form a loop around the bollard (2). The resulting formation will be under tension (3). Take hold of the end and make another loop, dropping that over the bollard (4, 5, 6). Hold the end tight and the knot will tighten on its own.

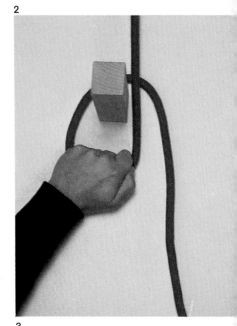

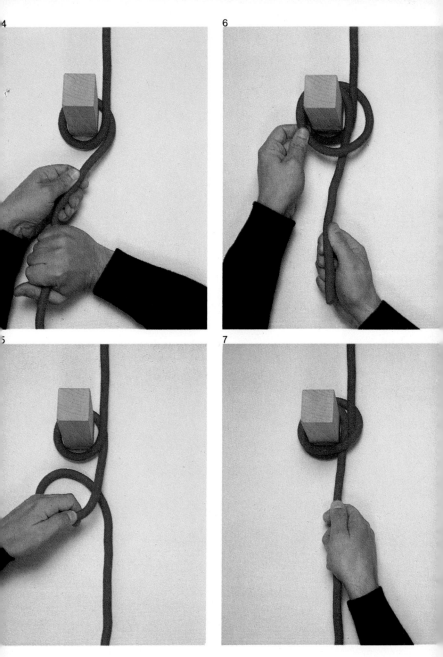

DOUBLE OR TRIPLE CLOVE HITCH

The double clove hitch is used when the knot is to be used for a long time without being checked, particularly when mooring a boat to a quay.

Method
Allowing a long enough end to make as many turns as required for safety, make a loop with the end underneath and drop it over the post (1). Repeat this operation as many times as desired (2).

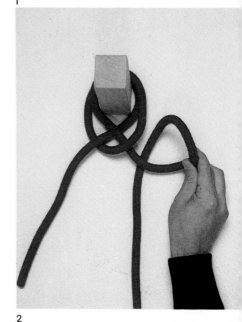

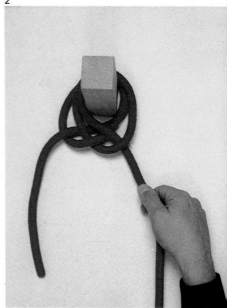

BILL HITCH

The bill hitch shown in this photo sequence is made with large-diameter rope and is useful when the knot has to be made and untied quickly.

Method
Pass the rope forward through the mouth of the hook (1); then wind the end around the hook to form a simple knot (2). Pull the standing part and the knot will automatically set itself tight (3).

2

1

3

CAT'S-PAW

This is the best hook knot for medium-diameter rope, as the strain is equal on both sides.

Method
Form two loops and twist them three or four times clockwise under equal tension (1, 2). Pass the two loops over the hook (3). The knot is tightened by pulling the standing parts.

COW HITCH

This knot, known also as the lanyard hitch, is usually made on a ring or post and is often used to tether animals temporarily. It is not a secure knot unless the tension on the two ends is equal, so its uses at sea are limited.

Method
The end is inserted into the ring from above (1). Passing in front of the standing part and crossing it, the end is then inserted into the ring again from underneath (2). Finally, the end is passed through the bight parallel to the standing part (3). Pull the standing part to tighten the knot.

2

1

3

HALF HITCHES

Half hitches are temporary knots which are not intended to support a lot of strain. They are used to complete and make other knots stronger, for hanging, tying, and hooking objects, etc. The half hitch is one of the best known knots and is widely used in all kinds of situations; it is used by housewives, butchers, builders, and carpenters. In sailing, half hitches are used to complete the fisherman's bend on head and reef earings and on all temporary fastenings.

The difference between the half hitch and the single hitch is that the former is tied around its own standing part whereas the latter is tied around an object.

Method
The end is passed into the ring from below and then behind the standing part and into the eye of the loop (1); the first half hitch is complete. Continue the same operation to form the number of half hitches desired (2, 3), remembering to tighten them one at a time.

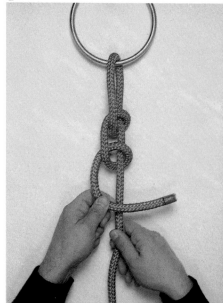

SLIPPED HALF HITCH

This is a variation on the simple half hitch. Because it is slipped it is easier to cast off, particularly when the rope is under strain, since pulling the end automatically releases the knot (4). Sailors use the slipped half hitch for head and reef earings.

4

FISHERMAN'S BEND

1

60

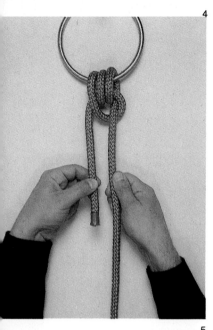

4

Also called the anchor bend, this is one of the most secure and widely used hitches. It is used by sailors for mooring at the wharf and to tie the anchor ring, a use from which it derives one of its names.

The fisherman's bend is normally made in small- and medium-diameter rope, as it is difficult to make in large-diameter rope.

Method
The end is passed through the ring two or three times from the bottom upwards without twisting the rope (1, 2). The end is then passed behind the standing part and is inserted through the turns around the ring (3, 4). The knot is now finished, but one or two half hitches are usually made around the standing part for greater security. Tighten them individually for a better hold (5).

If the ring is very fine compared to the rope it is better to make three or four turns.

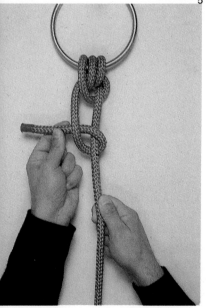

5

ROLLING HITCH

The rolling hitch, formerly known as the Magnus or Manger's hitch, is the best knot for bending a small rope to a larger one under strain and is used both at sea and in climbing. The knot can be slid along the heavier rope when the lighter line is perpendicular to it, but the knot tightens as soon as there is any lateral strain on the lighter rope. It was formerly used by sailors to hoist the yard horizontally and to uncoil the hawsers from the anchor capstan. In climbing, a similar knot, the Prusik knot, is made in a loop and is used on the ascent rope.

1

4

Method

Take two turns with the lighter rope around the heavier one working downwards (1). Then pass the end over the standing part and make a half hitch around the heavy rope above the first two turns. The end should be parallel to the standing part (2, 3). Pull the standing part downwards, and the knot is secured (4).

5

SLIPPED ROLLING HITCH

The hitch is slipped to make the knot easier to untie. This is done by making the final tuck with a bight instead of the end (5).

HIGHWAY- MAN'S HITCH, OR DRAW HITCH

The highwayman's hitch is alleged to have been used by highwaymen to tie up their horses. One pull on the end and the hitch was undone. It is a very simple knot, both to make and to untie. Tension on the standing part, however, will not undo the knot, and it is useful in various situations, such as lowering objects and making temporary fastenings.

1

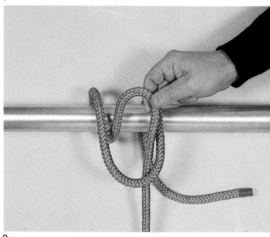

2

Method

Make a bight by folding back a long end and bend it over the post (1). Reaching through this loop, pull up the standing part in a bight and pull it tight (2, 3). Holding the bight secure with the right hand, form yet another loop (this time in the end) with the left hand (4) and pass this through the previous loop (5). Pull the standing part to tighten the knot (6). To untie it, you need only pull the end.

6

CONSTRICTOR KNOT

This is a simple and secure binding knot, but if it is pulled too tight it is hard to untie.

Method
Take two turns with the rope, making an overhand knot in the second (1, 2, 3). Thread the left end under the first turn and tighten (4, 5).

1

3

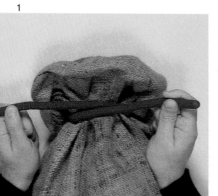

2

4

loops

Knots made into the end of a rope by folding it back into a loop or an eye and knotting it to its own standing part so that it is fixed and does not slide are called loops.

Unlike hitches, which are made directly onto an object and follow its shape, loops are made in the hand and are dropped over the object. These knots are indispensible to sailors, particularly the bowline which is used in many different situations. The main loops are the bowline, the bowline on a bight, the jury mast knot, the Spanish bowline, the true-lover's knot, the crown, angler's loop and the artillery knot.

The illustration on the following pages shows:
1. Bowline   2. Portuguese bowline   3. Three-part crown
4. Artillery loop   5. Spanish bowline   6. Bowline on a bight
7. Angler's loop   8. Jury mast knot

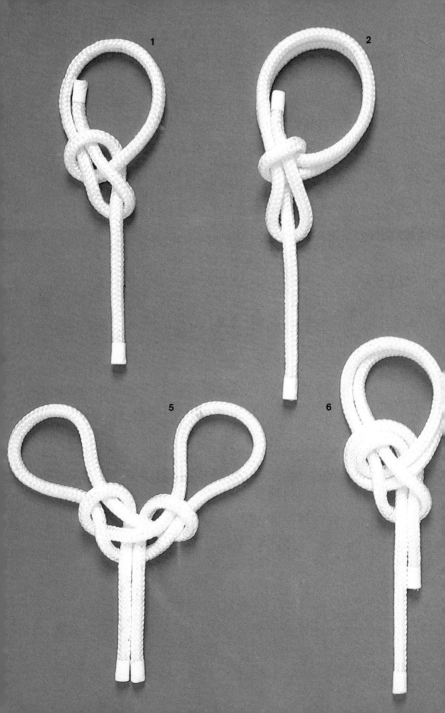

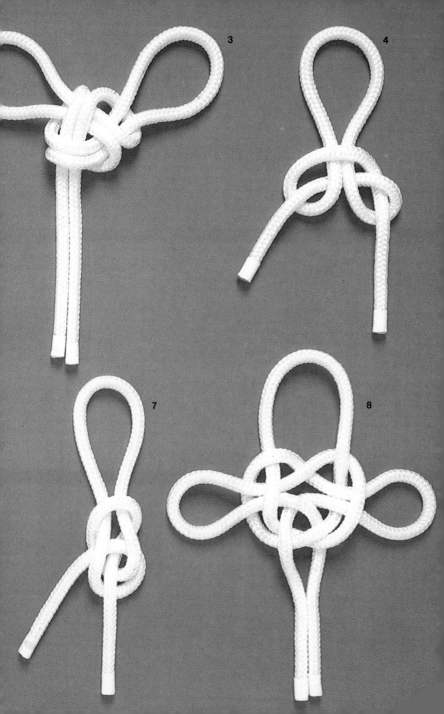

BOWLINE

Loop method

The bowline is the knot best known to sailors and is the most important in seamanship. There are numerous advantages to using this knot as it does not slip, come loose, or jam, and it is not difficult to untie when the rope is under strain.

The bowline is normally used to fix a rope to an object or to form a fixed loop at the end of a rope. It is used at sea on running rigging and for hoisting, joining, and salvage work. In climbing it is known as the Bulin knot and is used as a safety measure during the ascent when it is clipped into the karabiner.

2

3

1

Form a turn in the standing
part (1), and insert the end
into it from below (2). Pass
the end behind the standing
part and bring it back through
the turn (3, 4). Hold the end
and the loop with the right
hand and pull the standing
part to tighten the knot (5, 6).

SLIPPED BOWLINE

This is made by using a bight
for the final tuck (7).

Of course, before
beginning the slipped
bowline you must ensure that
the end is long enough. Tied
in this way, the bowline is
easier to untie if it is under
great strain.

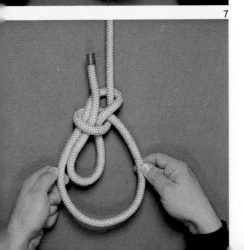

BOWLINE

Casting method

This is used when the bowline is to be tied around an object.

Method
Tie an overhand knot and pull the end to form a threaded eye in the standing part (1, 2, 3). Pass the end behind the standing part and insert the end back into the eye (4, 5). Hold the end in the loop with the left hand (6) and pull the standing part with the right hand to tighten the knot (7).

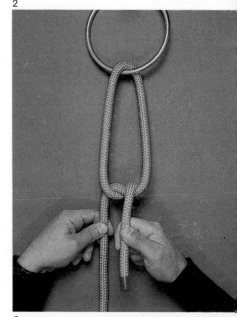

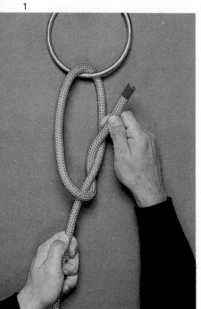

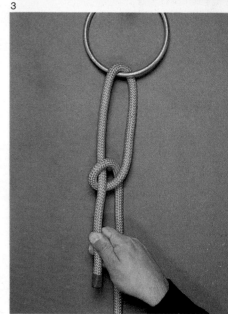

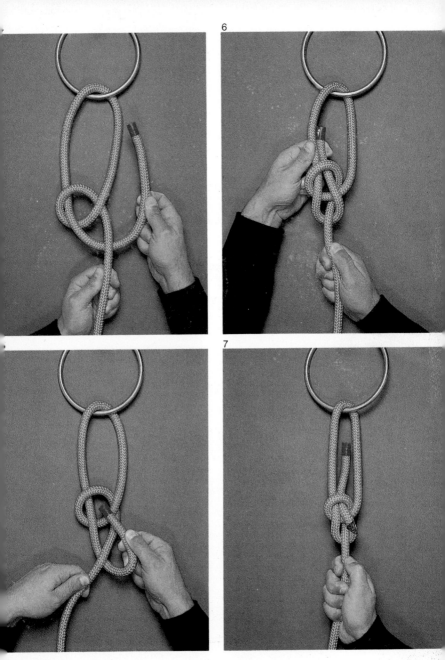

BOWLINE

Two-fingered method

This method is used when the bowline has to be made in a rope coming down from above or in front of whoever is making it.

Method
Form a loop by crossing the end over the standing part (1). Hold the two securely and twist the right hand clockwise to form a turn in the standing part (2, 3, 4, 5, 6). Twist the wrist carefully so that the end stays in the center of this turn. Then pass the end behind the standing part and insert it back in the turn (7, 8). Hold the end and the loop of the bowline securely in the right hand and pull the standing part with the left hand to tighten the knot (9).

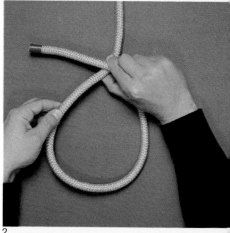

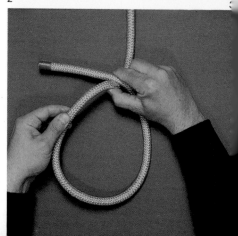

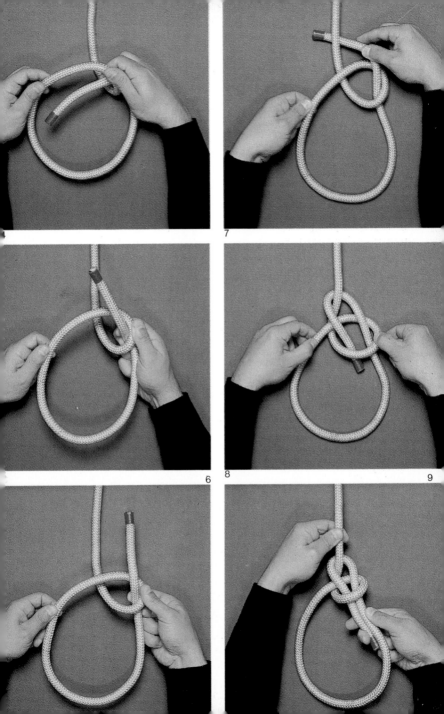

BOWLINE

One-handed method

This method is used in situations when only one hand can be used. The most important example of using a bowline made with one hand is rescuing someone from the sea. Having caught the lifeline thrown to him the person in trouble has to pass it around his back and make the knot as quickly as possible so that the rescuer can continue to pull him in.

Method
Holding the end in the right hand, cross it over the standing part (1). Make a clockwise turn in the standing part and slip your wrist through it (2, 3, 4), then pass the end behind the standing part (5). (As this move is quite difficult, it is advisable to practice it a number of times until it comes naturally.) Let go of the end for a moment and pick it up again on the other side of the standing part (6). Jerk the rope sharply towards you to pass the end through the turn (7), and immediately grasp the end and the loop (8). The tension on the standing part tightens the knot (9).

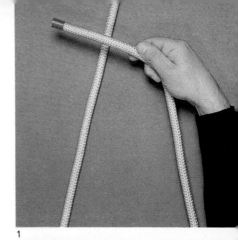

1

2

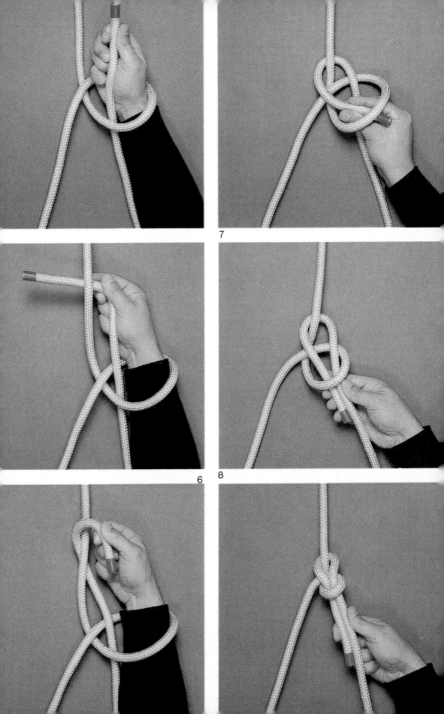

7

6 8

BOWLINE

Climber's method

Whereas the sailor makes the bowline in his hands and then drops it over the object, the climber ties this knot directly around his waist so that he can adjust the length correctly as a safety measure before tackling an ascent.

Method
Take the standing part of rope with the left hand and form the turn by pulling the rope towards you and twisting the wrist clockwise (1, 2, 3). Thread this turn over the wrist and take hold of the standing part again (4). Pull the standing part towards you through the turn, forming an eye through which you pass the end. Having done this, pick up the end again with the right hand (5, 6, 7). Insert the end back through the turn, holding the standing part in the left hand (8). Hold both the end and the loop securely and pull the standing part with the left hand to tighten the knot (9).

1

2

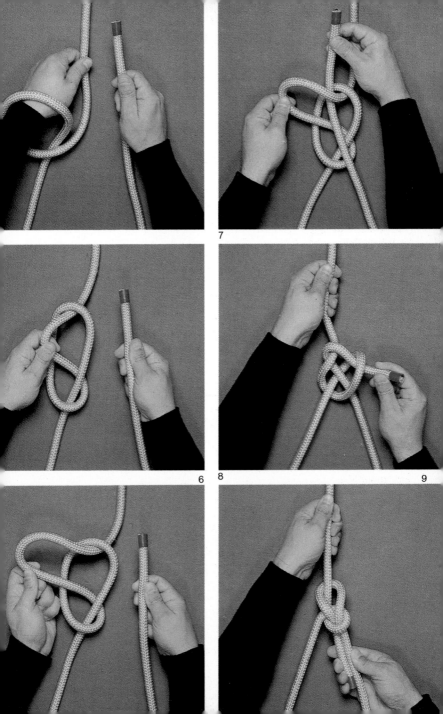

7

6 8

9

BOWLINE

With a rope under tension

This is used by sailors to hold
a boat.

Method
Make a simple knot and pull
the end to form a turn in the
standing part (1, 2). Pass the
end behind the standing part
and insert it through the eye
(3, 4). Now pass the end over
the standing part and insert it
into the loop just formed by
the end (5, 6). Give the end a
sharp pull upwards to form
the bowline (7).

2

1

3

PORTUGUESE BOWLINE

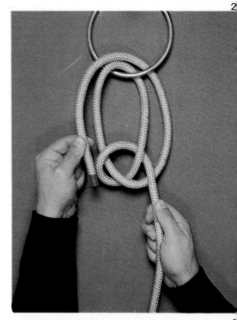

2

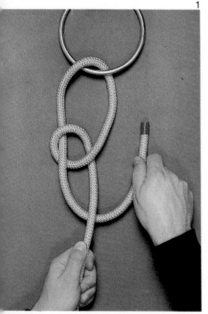

1

3

4

The Portuguese bowline is used by Portuguese sailors for tying the anchor. It is also known as the caulkner's bowline and is used to support a man who has to work from a suspended position. In this case, the first loop passes around the man's back; then having adjusted the two loops, he can sit on the second. The Portuguese bowline is useful for reinforcing the hold on an object, particularly if it is heavy. It can be formed with two or more loops, the more loops the stronger the knot.

Method
Form a turn on the standing part of the loop with the casting method described on page 72 (1). Pass the end behind the standing part and form a second loop (2). Insert the end into the turn (3); then pass the end behind the standing part again and insert it back into the turn (4). To tighten the knot, take hold of the end, and the two loops with the left hand and pull the standing part with the right hand (5).

5

BOWLINE ON A BIGHT

The bowline on a bight is made of two fixed loops which have the same diameter and overlap each other, but when opened out they can be used separately. It is a very old knot but is still used particularly in sea rescues. If the person to be rescued is conscious he puts one leg through each loop and holds

3

1

2

4

on to the standing part. If he is unconscious both legs are put through one loop and the other is placed under his armpits. As well as being used for rescue work, the bowline on a bight is used as a very safe method of salvaging objects.

Method
Double the end into a bight and overlap the standing part to form a loop (1). Using the two-fingered method (see page 74) form a loop (2, 3), then thread the bight through the loop and bend the bight back over the end of the loop to stop it widening (4, 5). Continue bending it back right around the loop until it comes up to the standing part again (6, 7). Be careful throughout the entire operation not to confuse the loop and the bight, which has to be pulled tight. The knot is worked by pulling the standing parts and the eye of the loop at the same time (8).

8

SPANISH BOWLINE

First method

This ancient knot is known to the sailor as the Spanish bowline and to the fireman as the chair knot. It is used in various situations for rescuing men from the sea and hoisting objects in a horizontal position, e.g., ladders, axles, etc. The knot is made up of two separate and

3

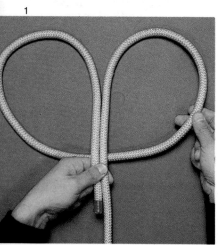

1

4

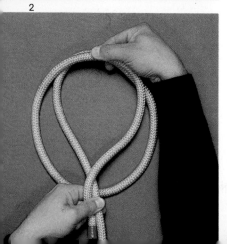

2

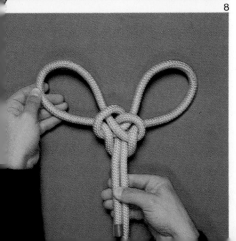

independent loops which hold well and are very safe even under great strain. Made in heavy rope the Spanish bowline can support the weight of scaffolding.

Method
It is easier to make the knot on a level surface if this is possible. Form two loops by doubling a bight and allowing it to drop back. There will now be a double standing part lying in front of the two loops formed (1). The left loop goes over the right (2) and both are then folded over the standing parts to form four small eyes (3). Hold these securely with the left index finger and pass the outer eyes through the inner ones (4, 5). This is done by reversing the eyes with a half twist of the wrist. Put the left thumb through the two eyes formed, which now point sideways (6). Tighten the knot by pulling the end, the standing part and the two eyes at the same time (7). The finished knot has two independent loops (8).

SPANISH BOWLINE

Second method

The Spanish bowline is easier to make with this method, as the steps are simpler but give the same end result.

Method
Make a bight near the end of the rope and bend it back to touch the double standing part, thus forming two loops (1). Twist the right loop by moving the wrist inwards (2) and repeat the same operation with the left loop (3). Thread the left loop through the right from below (4). Note that you now have a third loop at the bottom from which the double end comes out (5). Grasp the third loop with your right hand and twist your wrist clockwise to form a new loop which is then inserted in the larger right loop (6). Repeat this step on the left side (7). Hold the two side loops with the left thumb and pull the double end with the right hand (8). When the knot is drawn taut it should have two separate loops which are both tightened at the same time with the double end coming out parallel from the bottom (9).

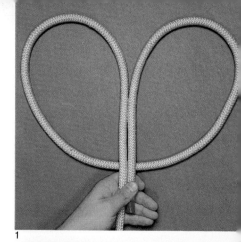

1

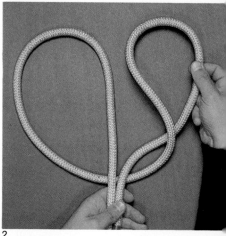

2

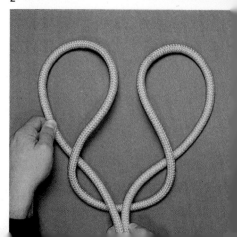

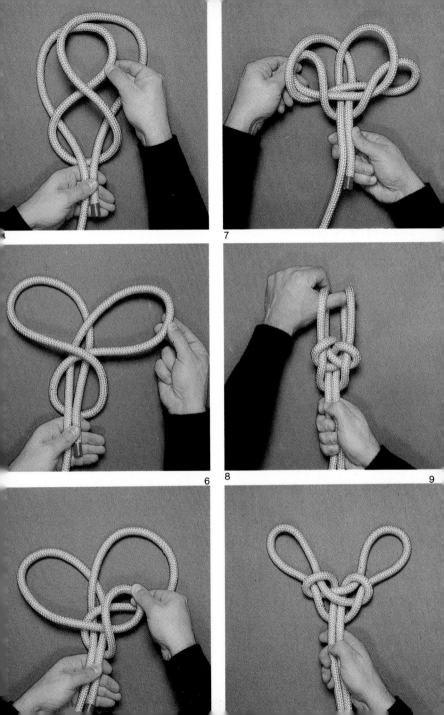

JURY MAST KNOT

This knot, also known as the masthead knot, is useful to sailors as an emergency measure to rig a jury mast. The central loop is dropped over the mast and the shrouds and stays are fixed to the other three loops by sheet bends.

Method
Make a turn to form the central loop (1). Twist your hand counterclockwise to form the left side loop (2) and clockwise to form the right side loop (3). Lace the left loops through the central loop, sliding it first over and then under the left edge of that loop. Slide the right loop under the right edge of the central loop (4, 5). The result should look like figure 6. Be sure all crossings are as illustrated. Take hold of the innermost loop by passing the index and middle finger of the right hand under then over the turns and the left hand over then under the turns (7, 8). Continue to pull sideways to form the two side loops. Pulling the central loop finally tightens the whole knot (9).

1

2

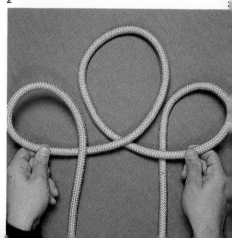

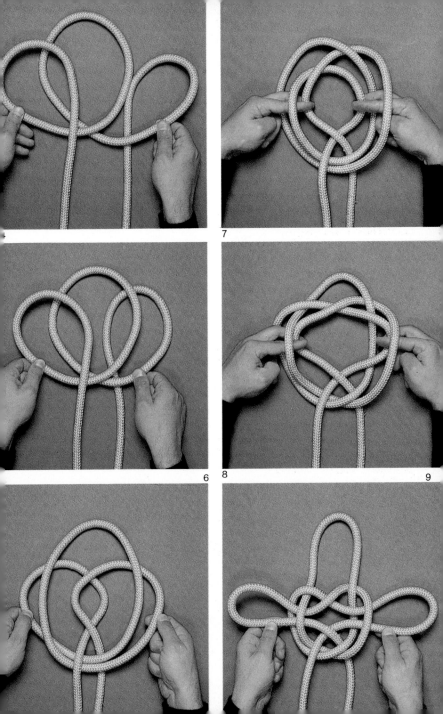

TRUE-LOVER'S KNOT

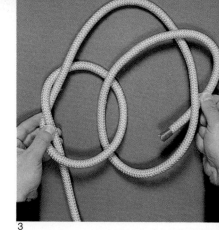

3

1

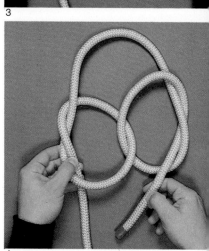

4

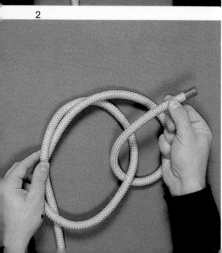

2

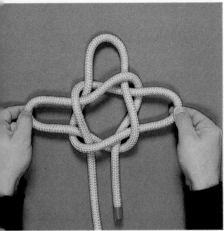

This knot, called the cross knot by sailors, is known only as a decorative knot, but it has a good grip when pulled tight and could be used instead of the jury mast knot if made in strong rope. It is used decoratively on bags and purses, and if worked in tape or ribbon it can produce imaginative results.

Method
Form an overhand knot, leaving a very long end (1). Hold the knot vertically and make a second overhand knot on the right side (2, 3). Form the third loop at the top by pulling the turn connecting the two knots (4). Insert the index and middle fingers into where the side knots are intertwined to get hold of the ends of the two eyes at the point where they intertwine (5, 6); pull them outwards to form the side loops which should be symmetrical (7). Tighten the side loops first, then the top one, making sure that all three are the same shape (8).

8

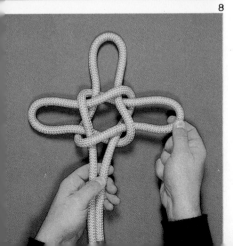

THREE-PART CROWN

This is a secure knot, but after it has supported a heavy weight it becomes difficult to untie; consequently it is not commonly used by seamen even though it is very sturdy. The three-part crown is used by campers to hang food and gear.

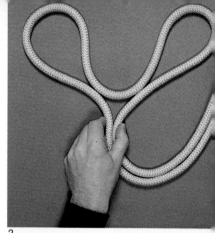

2

3

1

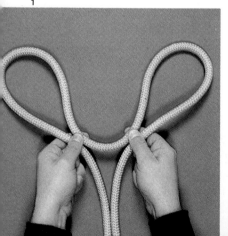

Method

Form two equal side loops by folding down a bight (1). Holding the bight closed with the left hand form a third loop beneath them with the right hand by moving the end and the standing part upwards in a counterclockwise direction (2). Still holding the base of the bight take the right side loop and turn it downwards (3, 4). Take the left side loop over the folded right loop (5) and insert it through the bottom loop (6). Pull both right and left loops to tighten the knot, taking care that both loops are equal (7). If they are not loosen the knot a little and pull the end of the smaller loop.

7

ANGLER'S LOOP

This knot is suitable for fishing line, string, or fine synthetic line and is used by fishermen to join the body of the line to the tip of the rod. It is also used by campers for hanging objects, as it does not slide and is very strong. It has the disadvantage of being difficult to untie, so it is not used at sea. The angler's loop made in small- and medium-diameter rope is rather bulky, but it is an interesting knot because of the ease with which it can be tied and its usefulness for some purposes.

1

2

Method
Form a bight near the end of the rope by moving the end counterclockwise, so the end lies beneath the standing part (1). Hold the bight with the left hand and make a large loop counterclockwise by passing the end behind the first loop (2). Make a clockwise turn around the base of the first bight with the end (3), and, keeping hold of the end, take the side of the second loop in the left hand and thread it through the bight (4, 5). Hold the standing part with the right hand while the left hand pulls up the loop to draw the knot tight (5, 6).

6

ARTILLERY LOOP

This knot is made in medium- and large-diameter rope and was formerly used by artillerymen to pull cannon and other artillery. It is also used by climbers, but in this case the loop must be large enough to slip over the shoulder, leaving the hands free for the climb.

Method
Form a large loop with the end under the standing part and pass the end up over the standing part to the left of the loop. Take the end of the loop with the right hand and twist it counterclockwise to form another loop (1). Turn this second loop upwards and insert it between the end and the left side of the upper loop (2). Tighten the knot by pulling both the end and the standing part at the same time (3).

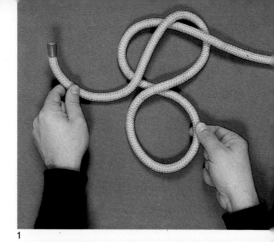

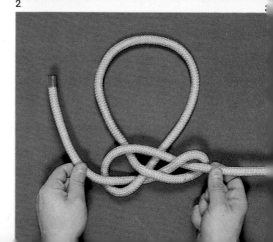

running knots

Running knots, also known as slip knots or nooses, are used in various situations, such as tying parcels or making traps and snares. Primitive man used running knots to make weapons and traps for capturing animals; so we can deduce that they are among the oldest known to man. These knots are divided into two groups, those formed by passing a bight through a fixed loop made at the end of the rope and those made with a closed bight knotted at the end or along the rope.

The main feature of running knots is that they tighten around the objects on which they are made; in fact the greater the strain on the end, the tighter the knot becomes around the object. On the other hand, when the strain is reduced, the knot slackens; so running knots are not used a lot in sailing.

The main running knots are the noose and the running bowline in the first group, and the Tarbuck knot and the hangman's knot in the second.

NOOSE

This is a simple knot which is rarely used at sea, although it is often used on land by campers and hunters to snare birds and small game. The noose is also used to put tackle cables under stress. It is made in small-diameter rope such as string and horsehair.

Method
Make a loop at the end of a rope, then take a turn with the end around the standing part to form a loop (1). Make an overhand knot in it with the end (2) and tighten the knot by pulling the end (3).

1

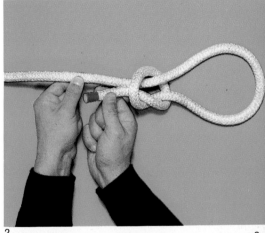

2

3

Left:
1. Noose
2. Running bowline
3. Hangman's knot
4. Tarbuck knot

RUNNING BOWLINE

The running bowline is mainly
used for hanging objects with
ropes of different diameters.
The weight of the object
determines the tension
necessary for the knot to grip.
It was used by poachers
during the last century but
also has many other uses; for it
is strong and secure, does not
weaken the rope, slides easily,
and undoes just as simply.
The running bowline is
probably the only running
knot used by sailors, who use
it on the running rigging or to
fish out floating objects that
have fallen overboard. It was
also used during the last
century for tightening the
squaresail to the yard in high
winds.

2

3

1

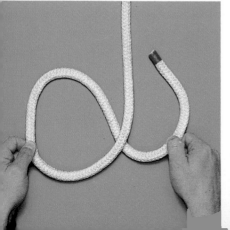

Method

Form a loop near the end of the rope (1) and then make a turn by moving the top edge of the loop from right to left (2). The end which is now under the standing part passes over it and is inserted through the turn (3, 4). Continuing in the same direction, pass the end under the eye of the loop and insert it once again into the turn (5, 6). Tighten the turn by pulling the end and the left side of the loop; then check that the standing part slides easily through the eye (7).

HANGMAN'S KNOT

Known as the hanged man's or hangman's knot, the use of this noose is obvious from its name. It slides easily without coming undone, withstands jerks, and can be made with a varying number of turns, provided an odd number are used (a minimum of seven; a maximum of thirteen).

3

1

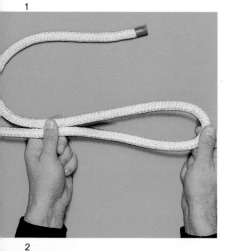

2

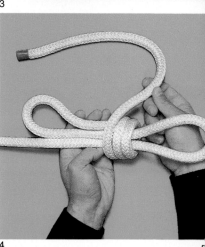

4

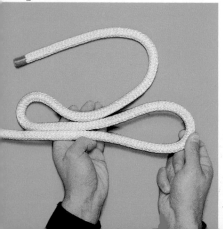

5

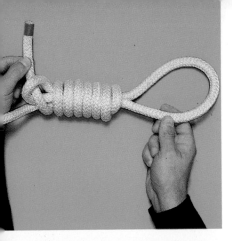

Method

Close a bight in the rope, leaving a long end (1). Make a second loop on the left side (2). Then take a number of turns (usually seven) around the loops, working the end from right to left (3, 4). Tighten the turns well one at a time and finish up at the eye of the second loop through which you pass the end (5, 6). To reach this point correctly, i.e., without having the end too long or too short, you have to calculate the length before you start. The knot is tightened by pulling the eye of the knot and then sliding the turns to the left to nip the end securely (7). Finally, check that the noose runs freely (8).

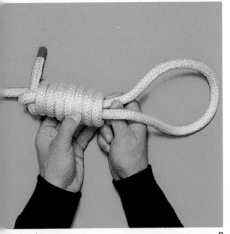

8

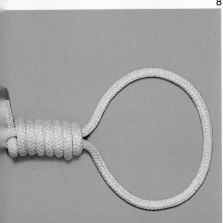

TARBUCK KNOT

This knot, developed for climbers, is used when the rope will be subject to heavy or sudden strains. It is easy to undo and does not chafe.

Method
Pass the end into the ring from below to form a loop; make a series of turns around the standing part towards the loop in a clockwise direction (1). Bring the end back down to the base of the turns and make another clockwise turn (2); then tuck the end back under itself (3).

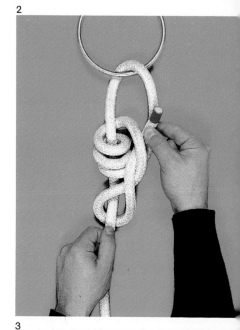

2

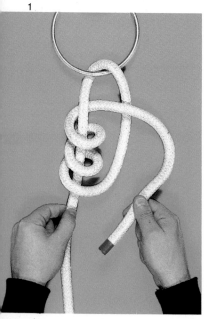

1

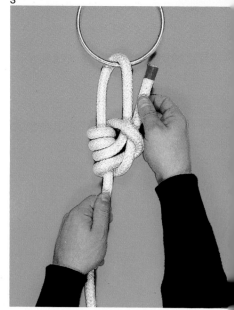

3

shortenings

When a rope is too long, shortenings are used to avoid cutting the rope and losing a lot of its value; as no knot uniting two ropes can have the same strength as an unbroken cord. Shortenings also eliminate any worn or damaged sections of rope; such weakened portions do not take any strain when they are incorporated into this kind of knot.

Shortenings can be used in many different circumstances, e.g., for hauling boats, loading goods, putting a rope under strain, salvaging damaged rope, and towing vehicles. They are also used, as suggested by their name, for varying the length of a rope to suit immediate requirements. The main shortenings are: the sheepshank, which is the most important in sailing; the loop knot, used by truck drivers, and the knotted sheepshank.

The illustration on the following page shows:
1. Loop knot 2. Sheepshank 3. Knotted sheepshank

LOOP KNOT

This simple knot is very important when you want to eliminate a worn section of rope; as the worn part is taken up in the dead point of the knot.

Method
Make a bight in the rope with the worn area in the center and make an overhand knot (1). Pull the ends to tighten the knot (2, 3).

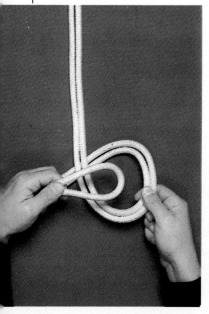

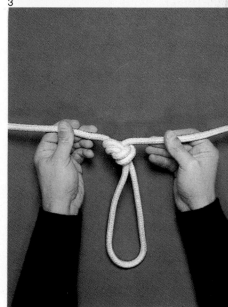

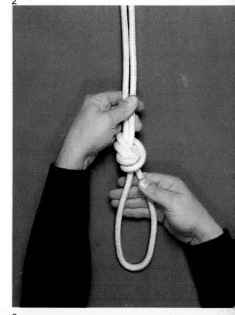

SHEEPSHANK

First method

The sheepshank belongs to the group of seamen's knots, and, like all the other knots that sailors use, it has certain special features: it does not chafe, unties easily after use, and has a good jamming action. It is used particularly in towing boats and on the running rigging. It does not alter shape, even if it has been left in use for a long time, and the rope does not wear, provided that the parts are under equal strain. The sheepshank is the best knot to use for considerably shortening a long rope. The number of half hitches made on the rope (a minimum of three and a maximum of five) determines both the grip of the knot and how much the rope is shortened.

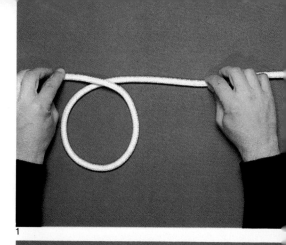

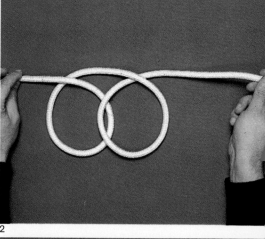

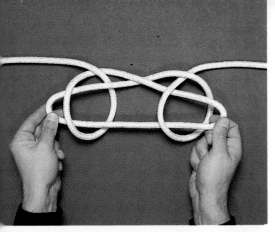

Method

Make the first half hitch by twisting the rope clockwise with the left hand (1). The second and third half hitches are formed slightly overlapping and with the same diameter as the first, and the rope running to the right must lie underneath (2, 3). The central half hitch is widened and pulled through the two lateral eyes (4); tighten these side loops and the knot takes its shape (5). Check the exact position of the half hitches; then pull the knot tight, being sure that the end loops are the same size (6).

6

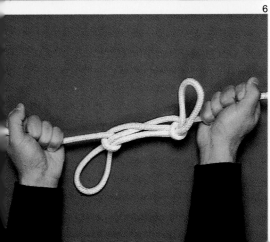

SHEEPSHANK

Second method

When tied in small-diameter rope this method is done in hand, unlike the first method which was made on a flat surface. The end result, however, is very similar. When using large-diameter rope or hawser, this is the method normally used. The large bights which begin the knot are run out on deck, and half hitches are formed around the ends. Sheepshanks are practical knots and are very useful when towing boats in confined spaces.

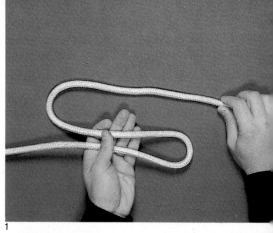

1

2

Method

Hold the rope in the left hand and take up the slack in the form of a letter S (1). Move the right hand counterclockwise to form a small loop (2); then thread the loop over the end of the first bight (3). Move the left hand counterclockwise to form a second loop (4) and thread this over the end of the second bight (5). Insert the right end in the small opening below the first bight. Reverse the small loop around the first bight. Tighten the knot by pulling the two ends at the same time and with equal force (6). It is good practice to check that the two bights are securely inserted in the respective eyes and that they are not too short; for if they do not protrude sufficiently they could come away and thus undo the knot.

6

113

KNOTTED SHEEPSHANK

This knot has the advantage over the ordinary sheepshank that it does not come undone but the disadvantage that it is more difficult to undo. It is not used much by seamen, as the two overhand knots that hold the knot together jam when subjected to great strain, making it very difficult to untie. It is, however, an interesting and useful knot when a permanent shortening is needed.

Method
Make a simple running knot, leaving a long end (1). Double the end back to the right and form an overhand knot in the end of the loop (2). Tighten the knot by pulling the ends (3).

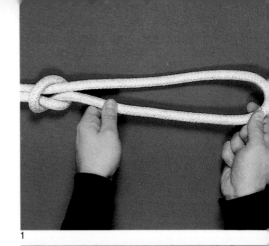
1

2

tackle

Tackle is a device used for lifting or moving weights; in its original form it was made up of a system of pulleys through which the force necessary to lift a specific weight was reduced. Tackle is used at sea for handling ropes or to reduce the strain on the running rigging and is a basic feature of sailing. To understand the importance of tackle, you need only remember that in a Force 5 wind (35 kph/22 mph) the pressure on the sails is 10 kg per sq m/2 lb per sq ft.

There are various types of tackle: a runner reduces the power required to lift a load by half, apart from friction; a gun or a luff tackle reduces it to a third; and winding tackle reduces it to a sixth. In general, it is not advisable to use a greater number of whips than this. While the effort needed to move a weight is reduced in proportion to the increasing complexity of the tackle, the time it takes and the amount of rope required increase.

SIMPLE AND COMPLEX TACKLE

A single whip with one pulley (1) does not reduce the effort required to lift a weight. A runner (2) divides in half the effort necessary to move a weight. Tackle with a double whip has the rope passing through two blocks, one standing and the other moving (3, 4). Rigged as here, it also reduces the effort to a half. This tackle is used on the boom sheet carriages of small sailing boats, by builders for hoisting concrete buckets or small loads, and to secure loads on roof racks.

The arrangement illustrated in figure 5 spreads the load

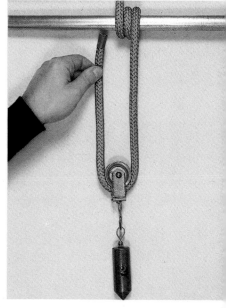

1

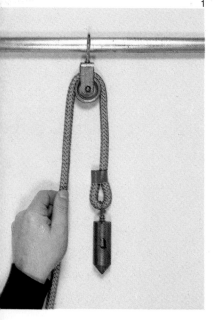

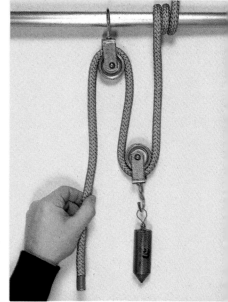

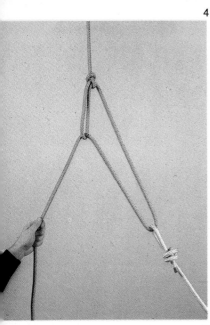

between two tackles and offers a significant increase in power. Similar to the Spanish burton, it is often used for the running rigging of an average tonnage sailing boat.

This kind of tackle was used by sailors in the past to make the stays of the fore and aft sails taut. The only disadvantage of complex tackle is that it is slow and requires a lot of rope. Consequently, it is practical only for short lifts.

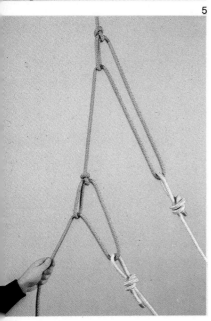

5

POLDO TACKLE

This is universal and can be used at sea and in climbing and camping. Poldo tackle is a truly ingenious device; thanks to the fact that it runs on a closed loop, it is self-locking.

Method
Make a bowline at one end of a rope. Run the other end through the loop of the bowline; then tie the end on itself with another bowline. The photographs (1, 2, 3) show the minimum and maximum extensions of the knot.
N.B. Man-made ropes should not be used for this knot by climbers.

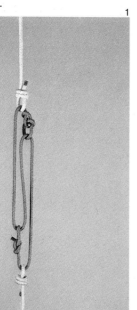

2

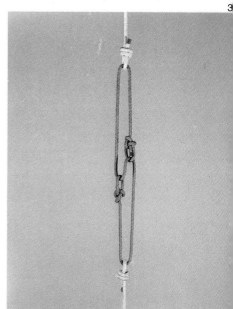

1

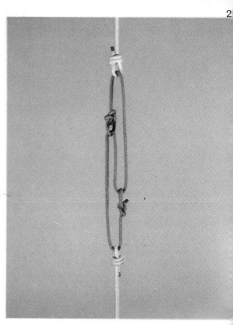

3

bends

Bends are used for joining two ropes at the ends to form a longer rope. These knots are divided into two groups: those made in string and small stuff which do not need to be untied after use (for example, the weaver's knot) and those which are to be untied after use. For bends to be secure, the ropes joined have to be of the same diameter and have the same properties. Also note that a wet rope is stronger than a dry one. The sheet bend is an exception to the above rule; as it is extraordinarily secure, even when made with ropes of different diameter. Bends should only be used as a temporary measure; splices should be used for more permanent joints. The most important bends are: the reef or square knot, the sheet bend, the carrick bend, the water knot, the grapevine knot, the Hunter's bend, the Japanese bend, and the surgeon's knot bend.

The illustration on the following pages shows:
1. Sheet bend   2. Japanese bend   3. Water knot
4. Reef or square knot   5. Hunter's bend   6. Carrick bend
7. Surgeon's knot bend   8. Grapevine knot

SHEET BEND

First method

Depending on the use to which it is going to be put, this knot has various names: the sheet bend when it is used to tie the sheets to the cringles on the ends of square sails and the flag bend when it is used to join the two corners of a flag to the rope used for hoisting or lowering it. This knot is one of the few good for uniting two ropes of different diameters and types. The sheet bend also has the interesting property that the greater the strain put on the ropes, the better the jamming action. It is quickly made and easily untied and is one of the basic knots that a good sailor should know.

1

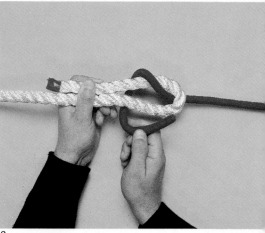

2

Method

Form a loop in the heavier rope and hold it secure in the left hand while introducing the lighter rope into the loop with the right hand (1). Bring the end of the lighter rope around and behind the loop of the heavier rope (2); then pass the end under its own standing part (3). Pull the standing parts of both ropes sideways to tighten the knot (4).

SLIPPED SHEET BEND

The slipped knot is easier to untie when the rope is under heavy strain. The knot is slipped by inserting a bight between the loop on the heavier rope and the standing part of the lighter rope (5).

6

DOUBLE OR TRIPLE SHEET BEND

Doubling the knot makes it more secure. It is done by making two or more turns around the heavier rope with the lighter rope (6).

SHEET BEND

Second method

This method is used in weaving, and when the sheet bend is tied this way it may be known as the weaver's knot. It is very quick to tie and is better made in string or twine.

Method
Cross the two ropes with the heavier rope over the lighter; then hold them together with the left hand and grasp the standing part of the lighter rope with the right hand (1). Form a loop with the standing part by twisting it clockwise with the right hand; the standing part should be behind its own end (2). Continue the turn to 360°; then leave the standing part running free (3). Take the end of the heavier rope in the right hand and form a bight to put into the eye formed by the lighter rope (4). Pull the ends of the two ropes and the knot begins to take shape (5). The end of the smaller rope is turned down by a twist of the standing part, and the knot is pulled tight (6). As can be seen in the sequence of photographs, this knot,

1

2

unlike the right-hand sheet bend, is made with just two essential hand movements, so it is easier to use for making sheet bends in series.

6

LEFT-HAND SHEET BEND

Somewhat less secure than the sheet bend, this is still a useful knot. It is often used by weavers and lace makers. It may be begun in the same way as a reef knot.

Method
Make a turn with the heavier rope around the lighter rope and cross the ends above; the end of the heavier rope should lie over the end of the lighter rope (1). Turn the end of the lighter rope down and pass it under its own standing part (2). Pull the standing parts to tighten the knot (3).

1

2
3

THIEF KNOT

The thief knot is very similar in appearance to the reef or square knot. The main difference is that it does not consist of two half knots. According to legend, sailors on whaling ships used this knot to tie their clothesbags, which were then retied by thieves with a reef knot.

Method
This little-used knot begins in the same way as the sheet bend. Form a bight on the end of one rope and introduce into it the end of the other (1). Make a turn around the bight and pass the end back through the original loop (2). Pull the standing parts to tighten the knot.

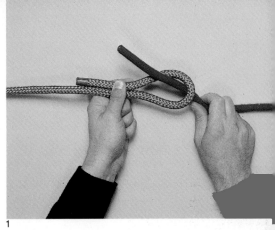

1

2

3

REEF OR SQUARE KNOT

This is the classic method for making the reef knot, which is one of the knots that a good sailor should know, even though it should only be used for making temporary joints in identical lines which will not be subject to strain. It consists mainly of a half knot followed by another, making sure that the standing parts come out on the same sides as the ends. It is generally made on small- and medium-diameter rope and is easy to remember because it is so simple.

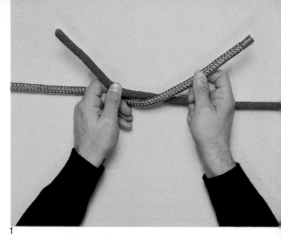

1

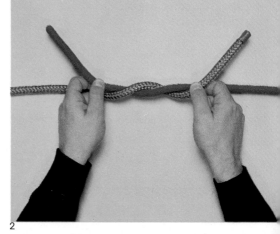

2

Method
Take a turn with the left-hand rope over and around the right (1, 2). Then cross the right end over the left to form a loop (3). The end below is bent forward (4) and is knotted over the other end in such a way that both ends come out on the same side as their own standing parts (5). Pull the ends sideways to tighten the knot.

SLIPPED REEF KNOT (SINGLE BOW)

To prepare for this knot leave one of the ends longer than the other. Fold this end into a bight and insert it into the turn. When tightened the knot holds the bight (6).

CAPSIZING A REEF KNOT

If greater strain is put on one end of a reef knot than on the other, it will capsize into an easily untied and insecure formation. Capsized reef knots have caused a number of accidents, which has given the knot a bad name. It is important that this knot be used only for the purposes for which it is suited.

Method
The reef knot can be capsized by taking one of the ends and pulling it in the opposite direction from which it came (1, 2). The knot slips and has no more grip, so you need only undo the end to untie the knot (3).

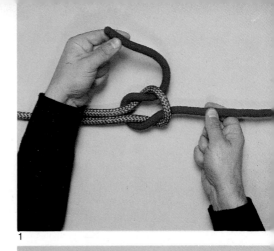

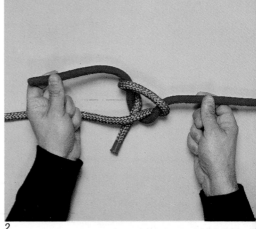

HUNTER'S BEND

This knot takes its name from its inventor who discovered it in 1978. It has an excellent grip and is very stable, and it is also very easy to untie. Its uses are similar to those of the sheet bend but it is bulkier.

Method
Form an overhand knot without pulling it tight and place it vertically. Take the end of the second rope and pass it through the eye of the turn to form a loop (1). Pass the end behind the standing part and insert it into the upper loop of the overhand knot, then through its own loop (2). Pull the two ends, which should protrude laterally from their respective knots. Pull the standing parts to tighten the knot fully (3).

1

2

3

SURGEON'S KNOT OR SURGEON'S KNOT BEND

When making sutures in a wound, surgeons use various knots such as the carrick bend, the reef knot, and the suture knot, which has become known as the surgeon's knot. It was discovered about half a century ago and seems to be the most suitable for the purpose. The surgeon's knot has an excellent grip and is flatter and less bulky than the other knots, which tended to produce visible and disfiguring scars. The surgeon's knot is a variation of the reef knot made by increasing the number of turns made in the two parts of the knot. It is less bulky but still secure if only one turn is taken in the top part of the knot.

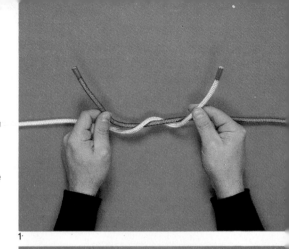

1

2

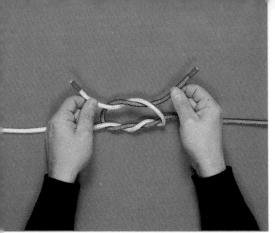

Method

Cross the ends and take one end down behind the other rope and up to the front again twice (1, 2). Point the ends upwards and cross them again, holding the right over the left (3). Now do the same as before to produce two turns on the bottom and two on the top (4, 5). Tighten the knot by pulling the ropes at the ends (6). If the turns are made well on each other, the knot will be very compact.

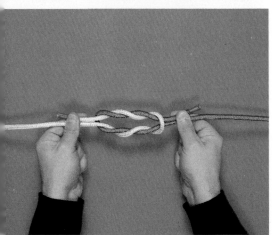

6

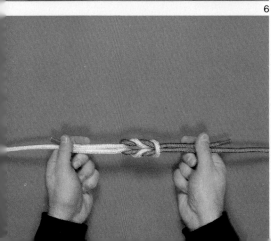

JAPANESE BEND

The Japanese bend, sometimes called a square knot, is a decorative knot and is used as the basis of other decorative knots. It is usually made in string or small stuff and is extremely attractive when made in series.

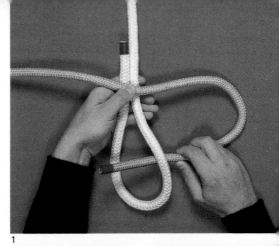

1

2

Method

Bend the end of one rope into a bight and hold it securely in the left hand. Take the end of the other rope in the right hand, pass it over the first rope, and thread it from below into the eye formed by the first rope (1). This will form two connected bights at right angles to each other (2). Bend the end of the right eye into another bight and insert it into the lower eye (3). The end of the original lower bight should now be inserted into the new left loop (4). The shape of the knot begins to appear (5). Check the various moves, then work the ends and the standing parts to tighten the knot (6). If you want to make a series of these knots, start with very long ends and repeat the above steps.

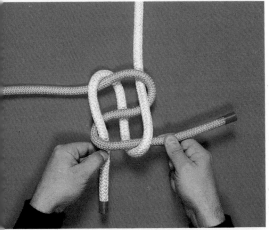

6

CARRICK BEND

This knot consists of two overhand loops crossing each other. It is known under various names: the split knot to the knitwear manufacturer, the warp knot to the sailor, and the cowboy knot to the cowhand. The carrick bend is a very secure way of joining two ropes of equal diameter but of different types. It is more stable than the reef knot, because it does not slip; but it is not commonly used at sea, because it becomes extremely difficult to untie if it has been subjected to great strain or if it is wet. It is used on large-diameter rope such as hawsers and warp ropes and is also used in climbing for joining two heavy ropes.

Method

Take the end of one rope and form a loop over the standing part, securing it with the left hand (1). Form a second loop with the other rope, passing it under the eye of the previous loop, then over the standing part and behind the end of that loop (2). Insert the end of the second rope into the loop of the first; then pass it behind its own standing part and draw it out of the loop (3, 4). Pull both standing parts at the same time to tighten the knot (5, 6).

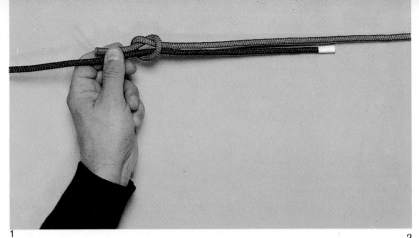

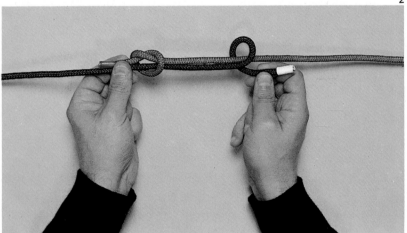

WATER KNOT

This knot was invented during the last century and is also known as the fisherman's, English, Englishman's, true-lover's, or angler's knot. It is made in string, line, or small-diameter rope and is a little bulky, but it is strong and therefore widely used by rod fishermen. It is a very simple knot made up of two overhand knots which jam against each other. It is not often used by sailors because it

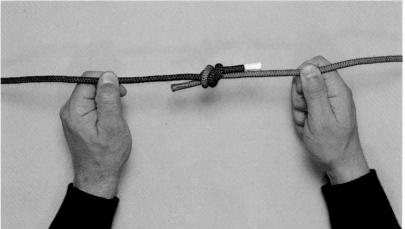

is not suitable for large- or medium-diameter rope and, in fact, the knot is not as strong as the rope itself when there is great strain.

Method
Lay the ends of two cords parallel to one another and make an overhand knot in one end around the other cord (1). Repeat this operation with the end of the other cord (2, 3). Pull the two standing parts so that the two overhand knots slide together (4). After the knot is made, one end should lie above the knot and one below.

GRAPEVINE OR DOUBLE FISHERMAN'S KNOT

This knot is particularly suitable for fishermen who use it on their lines for more secure joints. It is suitable only for thin line and string, because it is quite bulky. The grapevine knot is used by campers on tent guy ropes or to join lengths of string used for tying up or hanging objects, etc. It is also used by climbers on small stuff.

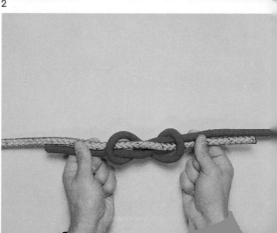

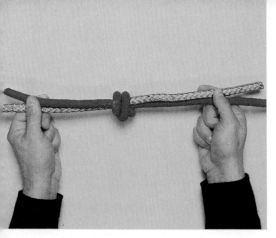

Method

To join the ends of the two ropes, pass the end of the first rope over the standing part of the second, forming a figure-eight knot (1). To close the knot, insert the end into the left loop (2); pull the end and standing part to tighten the first knot (3, 4). Make the second knot in the same way (5). If this proves difficult, you can turn the ropes over so that the second knot can be made in exactly the same way as the first. When the second knot has been tightened, the knots are brought together by pulling both standing parts (6). The grapevine knot, like the water knot, should have one end above the standing part and one below. If not, it means that the knot is not correct.

6

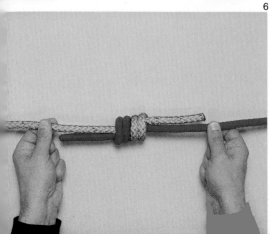

knots for the fisherman

Joining a hook to a line is an admirable work of ingenuity, imagination, and perfection. The result is a small, barely distinguishable lump of line drawn up into a neat, tight roll, hiding the experience gathered over thousands of years; so it should come as no surprise that there is such a variety of knots used for this purpose. The size of the hook, its shape, the type of line, and many other details, which may at first appear irrelevant, combine to tell the expert angler whether to use one knot or another to give him a perfectly harmonious fusing of hook and line.

There are basically two types of fishing hooks: those with an eye at the end and those without, and there are different knots for each of these types. Technically speaking, fishing knots do not constitute a new category but simply a regrouping according to the use for which they are intended. As we shall see, all hook knots fall into the categories that have already been discussed: they can be classified as stopper knots, hitches, loops, etc.

For the sake of clarity we have used large hooks and heavy rope in the illustrations in this chapter instead of the materials familiar to anglers. This will make the movements and the structure of the knots simpler to follow, but obviously a great deal of practice and subtlety of movement will be needed when working with small hooks and gut.

KNOTS FOR EYE HOOKS

First type

This knot is quick and easy to make and is not bulky, so it can be used for small and medium-sized hooks. It will withstand sharp jerks, but could give some problems if it has been used for a long time in conditions of uneven strain. For this reason it should be tightened very well.

Method
Pass the end through the eye of the hook and take a turn around its shank (1). Continue by passing the end over the standing part and inserting it into the loop (2). Tighten the knot by holding the end securely against the hook and pulling the standing part (3).

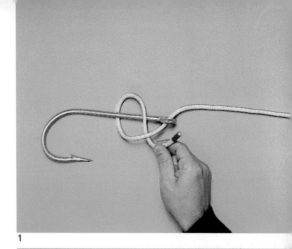

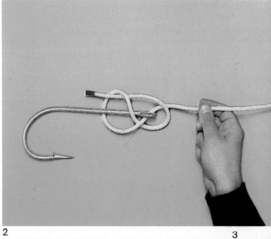

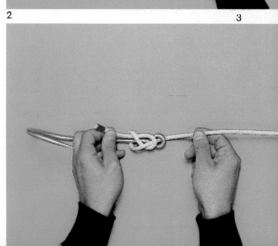

KNOTS FOR EYE HOOKS

Second type

This is another compact knot which is fairly universal. It can be used with any kind of hook and any type of single line and gives an excellent grip. The knot is made around the standing part of the line and the only point of contact between line and hook is the initial turn through the eye. This is the Achilles heel of the knot as it is here that the line generally breaks. This problem can be overcome by doubling the initial turn, i.e., passing the end twice through the eye. This increases the reliability of the knot, but it also increases its bulk and so limits its use to hooks of a certain size.

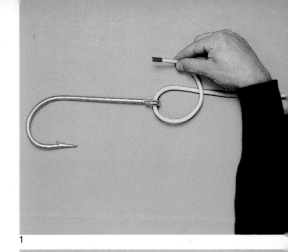

1

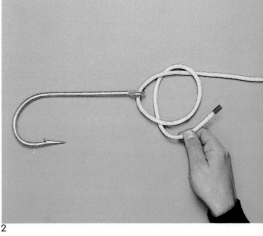

2

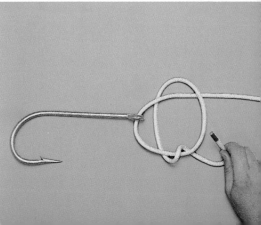

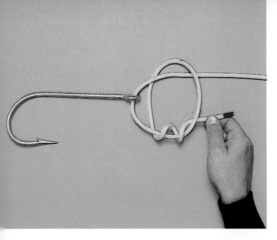

Method
This is quite an easy knot to make. Begin by taking a simple turn with the end of the line through the eye of the hook (1). Continue by taking a turn over the standing part (2) to produce a loop which is then held by a series of turns (3, 4). The number of turns here is up to you, although we recommend two or three at the most. The knot is finished at this point; to tighten it, hold the hook and pull the standing part (5), leaving the end free. The knot should be pulled tight gradually and smoothly, so as not to distort its inner order. Figure 6 shows the finished knot, with the end coming out in the same direction as the standing part.

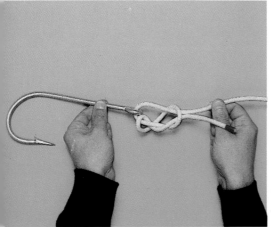

6

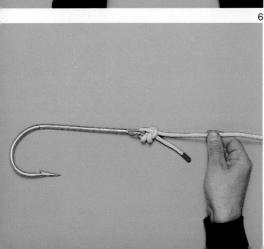

KNOTS FOR EYE HOOKS

Third type

This is a beautifully symmetrical knot which offers an excellent grip. Figure 5 shows the knot formed but still loose, so you can see the nearly symmetrical formation that makes it so very secure. The only undeniable disadvantage of this knot is that it is quite unhandy to make, particularly in the final stages. To make it easier, it is better to leave the turns quite large and then trim the end after the knot has been tightened. The loss of a little of the line will be compensated for by the fact that you do not have the problems that can arise from working with very small loops.

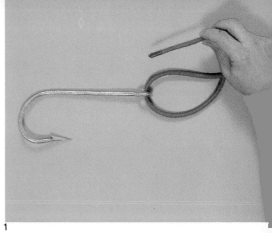

1

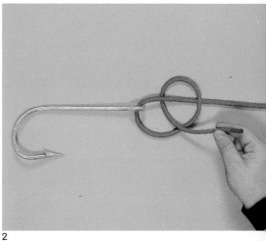

2

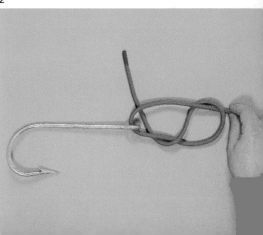

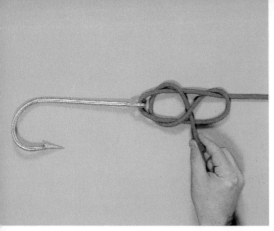

Method

Begin by making a loop through the eye of the hook (1). Turn the end downwards through the loop (2), then up again behind it (3), and down through it to make a figure eight (4). Make a turn through the bottom of the right loop of the eight (5) and tighten by pulling the hook and the standing part smoothly (6).

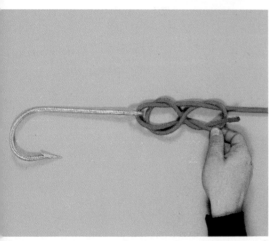

6

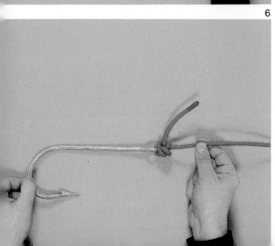

KNOTS FOR EYE HOOKS

Fourth type

This is a beautiful and universally used knot, but it is not simple to make. It is formed in two different stages: in the first the line is wrapped around the shank of the hook; in the second the turns that have been formed are transferred from the shank to the standing part with care, so that they remain in order. The resulting knot has an excellent grip and is admirably symmetrical.

Method
Begin by passing the end of the line through the eye of the hook and forming turns around the shank (1). The number of turns is entirely discretionary, but it is not a good idea to make too many. Although many turns make the knot more attractive, they also increase its bulk without having any effect on its grip. The next steps consist of passing the end in the opposite direction through the eye of the hook (2, 3). Now transfer the right-hand turn onto the standing part (4). Continue by

150

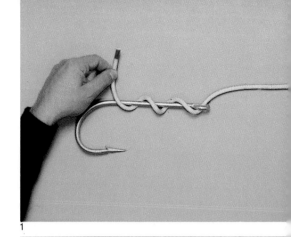

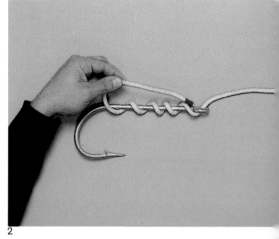

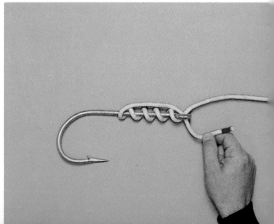

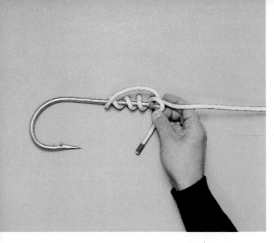

transferring the turns one by one onto the standing part, working from the left and passing each turn over the others (5). Take care when you do this to keep the turns in the same order on the standing part as they were on the shank of the hook, i.e., the turn on the far left of the hook will be on the far left of the standing part and so on until they have all been transferred. Tighten the knot by pulling both the hook and the standing part (6).

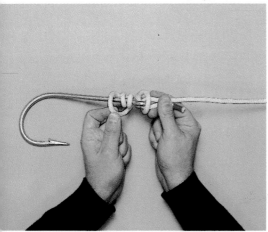

6

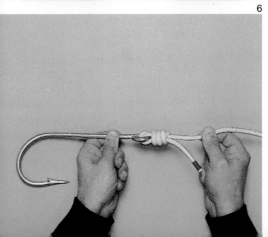

KNOTS FOR EYE HOOKS

Fifth type

This is quite a complex knot, which can be useful for tying small anchors or very large hooks with large eyes. Its special feature is that it is partially tied around the end of the hook so the grip is ensured not only by passing the line through the eye but also by the turns around the shank.

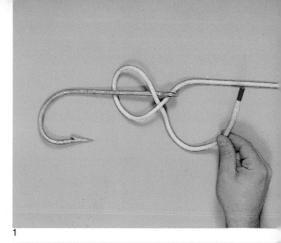

1

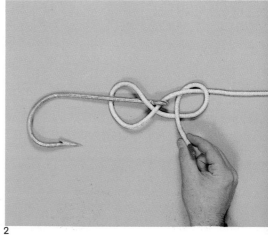

2

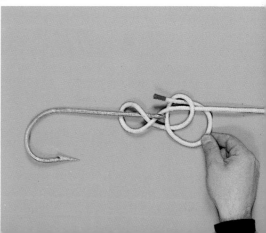

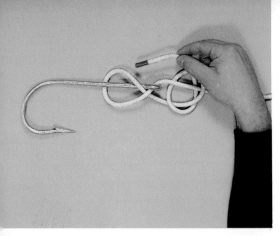

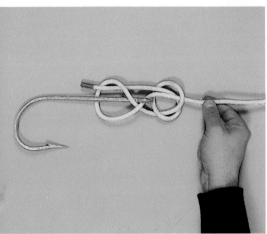

Method
Pass the end through the eye and take a full turn around the shank tucking the end (1). Then proceed to form part of the knot around the standing part: take a turn around the standing part and tuck the end (2); pass the end behind the standing part and insert it through the loop formed by the turn (3); then bring it back along the shank of the hook (4). Finish off the knot by inserting the end through the loop formed at the beginning around the shank of the hook (5). To tighten the knot, hold the end along the shank and pull on the standing part (6).

6

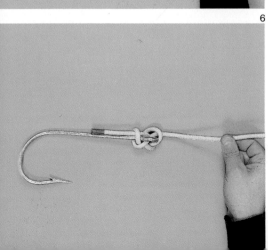

KNOTS FOR EYE HOOKS

Sixth type

Unlike the previous knots, which were either wholly or partly made around the standing part, this knot is made entirely around the shank. This feature gives the knot exceptional grip in all kinds of conditions. Its disadvantage is that the hook always tends to be at a slight angle to the line, which is why this knot is better used on large hooks or anchors.

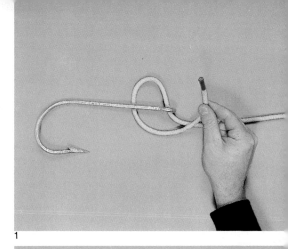

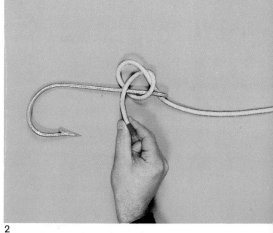

1

2

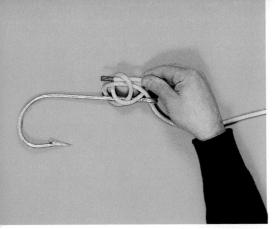

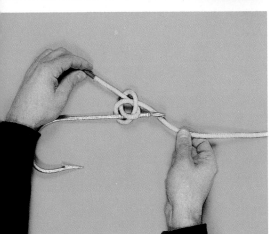

Method

Begin by passing the end through the eye of the hook to form a large loop (1). Insert the end into the loop from behind (2) and pass it upwards between the hook and the line (3). Finish off the knot by inserting the end through the loop thus formed (4), and tighten it by pulling the end and the standing part slowly and smoothly (5). The final result is shown in figure 6. You can see both the advantages and the disadvantages discussed above.

6

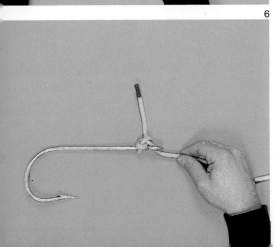

KNOTS FOR EYE HOOKS

Seventh type

This knot is similar to the previous one; it is formed entirely on the shank and not on the standing part. The turns close upon each other to give an excellent grip on the shank, but it should be stressed that the final result has at least two disadvantages: the knot is quite bulky and the hook tends to be at an angle to the line. It is recommended for small anchors or very large hooks.

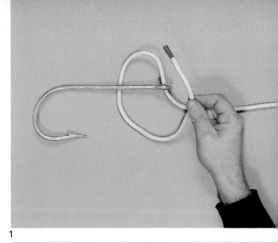

1

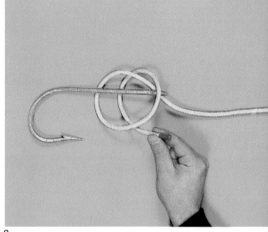

2

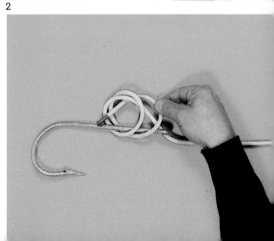

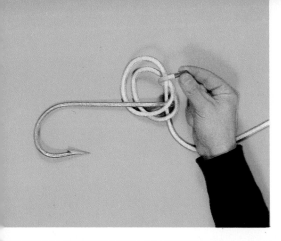

Method

First, pass the end through the eye from below; then pass it behind the hook to form the first turn around the shank (1). Form a second turn inside the first (2). The number of these turns can vary; as long as they all go in the same direction, you can have as many as you like. Remember, however, that the grip of the knot does not depend on the number of turns alone, while they do affect its bulk. Make a half turn into the turns formed so that the end wraps around them (3, 4); then close it on itself leaving the line issuing from the hook underneath (5). This completes the knot, which should be worked into the shape shown in figure 6.

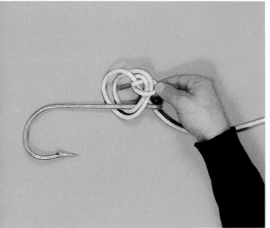

6

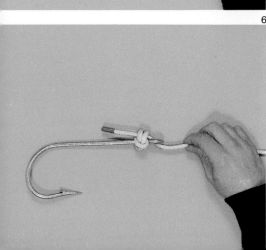

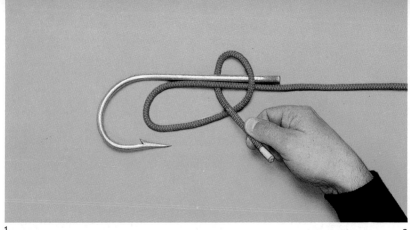

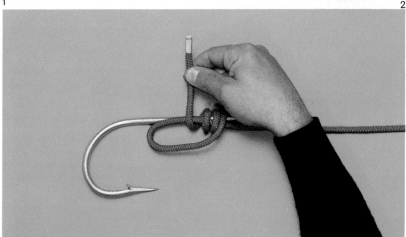

KNOTS FOR FLATTED HOOKS

First type

The knot shown here is the multiple overhand knot (see p. 38), which is generally classified as a stopper knot or as a weight for the end of a rope. In these roles it is considered to be a decorative knot, but in fishing it is one of the most popular knots for tying line to hooks which do not have eyes. It is also the basis for a wide range of variations.

Method
Place the line along the shank of the hook, bend it back, and take it around the shank and the standing part (1). Then make a series of turns around the shank and the standing part of the line (2, 3). The number of turns may vary, but remember

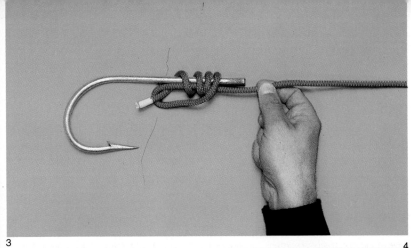

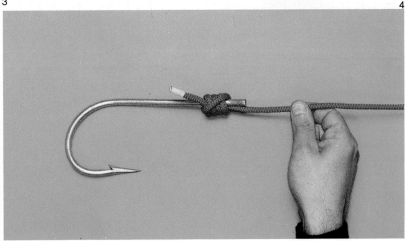

that although the knot is more
secure when there are more turns, it
is also more bulky. You will have to
find a balance between bulk and
grip on the basis of the shape of the
shank. Finish off the knot by pulling
the end and the standing part at the
same time, then pull the standing
part again (4). It is important that
the knot be drawn up tightly.

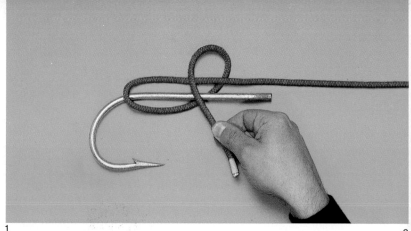

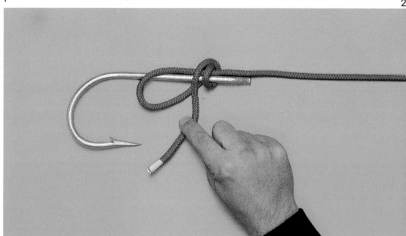

KNOTS FOR FLATTED HOOKS

Second type

This is a heaving line knot (see pp. 36–37), which has already been described under stopper knots, but it is also used to tie a line to a hook. It is easy and quick to make and is without a doubt the most popular knot used for flatted hooks.

Method

Lay the line along the shank and then bend it back to form a large loop (1). Next, make a series of turns, working from right to left and covering both sides of the loop and the shank (2). The number of turns may vary as needed. The expert angler will find the right compromise between bulk and grip when deciding how many turns to use. Finish off the knot by inserting

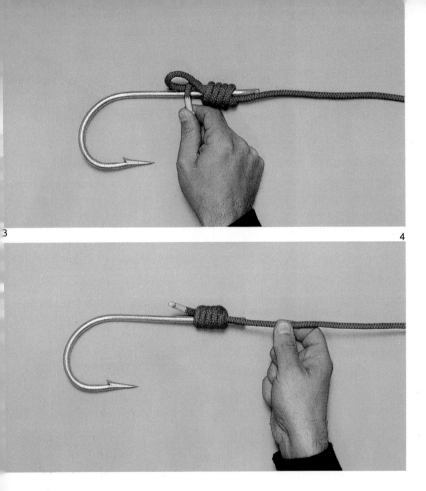

the end through the original loop
(3); then draw up the knot by
holding the hook tightly while
pulling the standing part (4). This
should be done very carefully.
Tightness and the number of turns
are the principal factors determining
the grip of the knot.

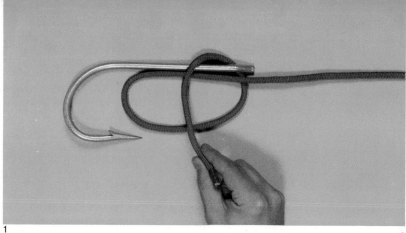

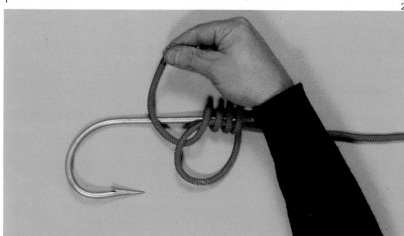

KNOTS FOR FLATTED HOOKS

Third type

This is an intelligent application of the fisherman's bend (see pp. 60–61) and is made around its own standing part and the shank of the hook. The result is somewhat bulky and so only suitable for hooks of some size or with a very prominent tad. The jamming action is not remarkable in itself and depends largely on the number of turns and how well the knot is drawn up. This last operation should be done in such a way as to put equal tension on all the turns, but this is not easy to do, as the knot tends to tighten more on the outer turns than on the inner ones.

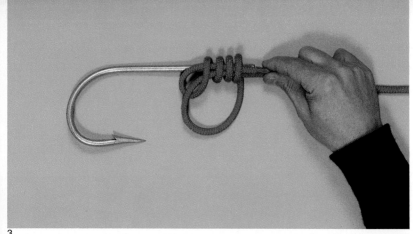

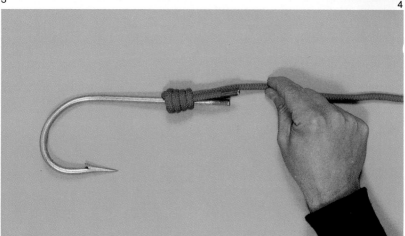

Method

Lay the line along the shank and form a loop (1); then make a series of turns around the shank and the standing part, working from right to left. Leave the turns rather loose (2). Finish the knot by passing the end back through the turns (3), and then tighten it by pulling alternately on the standing part and the end, taking care to keep the knot in the right position on the hook (4).

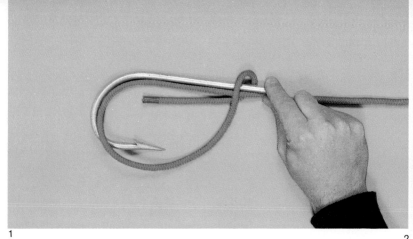

1

2

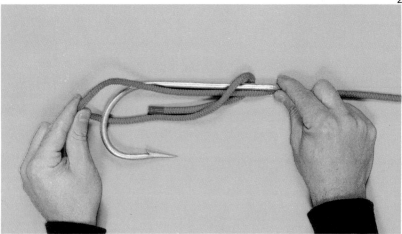

KNOTS FOR
FLATTED HOOKS

Fourth type

This is an unusual knot not only
because of its end result, which is
quite effective, but more because of
the way it is made. It is made
exclusively with a bight instead of
with the end like most knots. The
grip is good as long as there are

many turns and the knot is carefully
drawn up.

Method
Form a large loop in your line; the
end should pass behind the shank
of the hook and the standing part
and should end up parallel to the
shank (1). Half twist the bight and
pass it over the mouth of the hook
(2). Bring the side of the loop that is
behind the hook forward to form a

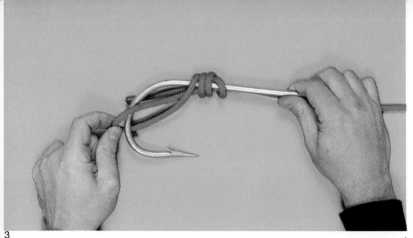

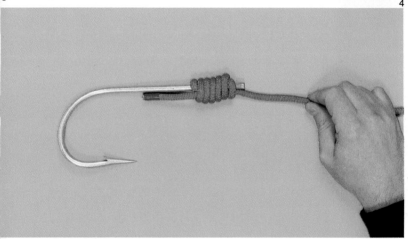

turn around the shank and end.
Repeat this operation until you have
the desired number of turns (3). The
size of the bight decreases as the
number of turns increases, so it
becomes necessary to move the
knot closer to the mouth of the
hook. This is helpful, partially
tightening the turns, which have
already been formed. Tighten the
knot by holding both the end and
the hook together and pulling the
standing part (4).

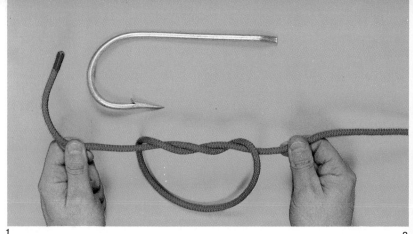

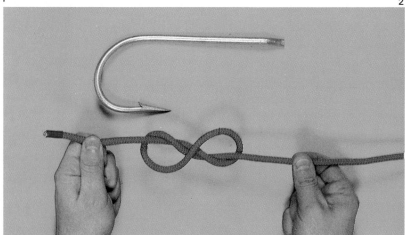

KNOTS FOR FLATTED HOOKS

Fifth type

This knot has great advantages but also great limitations. Among the former is the fact that it is extremely quick and easy to make because it is formed off the hook which is inserted and gripped only at the last moment when the knot is drawn up.

Another undoubted advantage is the fact that the knot is compact. However, set against these positive features is the fact that a good grip cannot be guaranteed unless it is used on hooks with a good-sized tad.

166

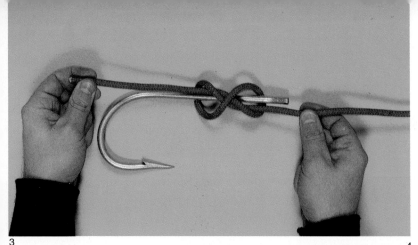

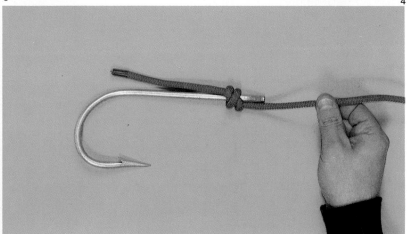

3

4

Method

Begin by forming a large loop through which you make two complete turns with the end (1). Pull the end and the standing part at the same time and the loop will form a figure eight, provided that the strain applied by each hand is as equal as possible (2). This completes the knot, which is now ready for the hook to be inserted. The shank is passed through the

figure eight that has been formed; it goes under the end and over the standing part (3). No particular care is needed when drawing up the knot; simply pull both the end and the standing part slowly and smoothly (4).

BARREL KNOT

This is a well-known knot, sometimes called the blood knot, which is used to join fine lines of equal diameter, such as gut. At first sight, it looks complicated to make but it is, in fact, the opposite. It is better to leave the knot rather loose while you are making it so that you do not confuse the turns, even though this means that the resulting ends will be too long and will have to be trimmed after the knot has been drawn up. The grip is excellent.

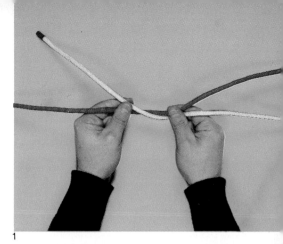

1

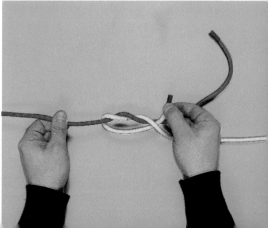

2

Method

Place the two ends alongside one another (1). Take the end to the left and make two turns around the other line (2). Now bend the left end back and insert it between the two lines at the point where they crossed initially (3). Repeat this process with the right end (4). The knot is now complete but loose (5); before pulling it tight, check that it is perfectly symmetrical. The knot can then be drawn up by pulling the ends and then the standing parts of the two lines (6).

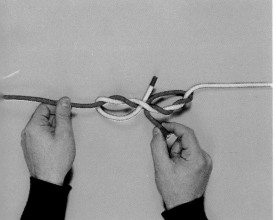

6

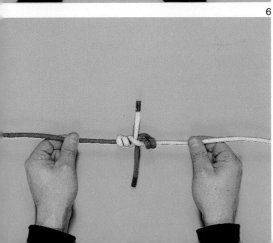

BRANCH
OR DROPPER
KNOTTING

Some kinds of fishing
require a number of
hooks to be tied in
series to one line, so
you need a system by
which you can bend a
series of shorter lines,
each with its own hook,
to the main line. There
are many branch or
dropper knots that will
accomplish this but the
following knot is popular
because it has a good grip
and does not unduly
damage the main line.

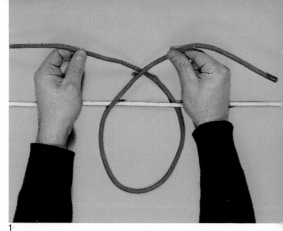

1

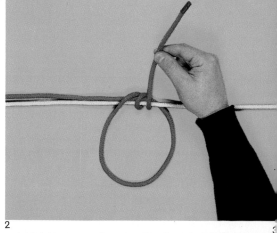

2

3

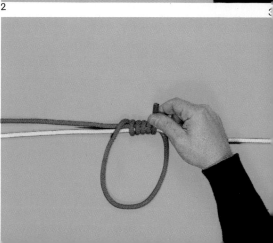

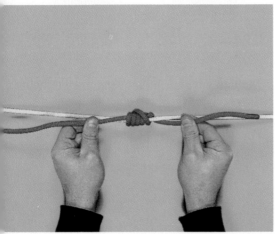

6

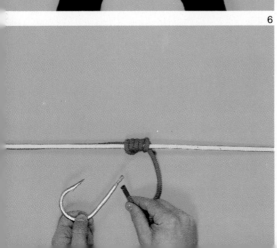

Method

Form a large loop around the main line (1). Then take a few turns through the loop and around the line with the end (2, 3), taking care not to let the turns overlap. As with most hitches, the grip of this branch knot is basically determined by a uniform internal distribution of the tension, so any overlapping of the turns would irreparably affect the grip and would allow the knot to slip along the main line. Pull the end and the standing part slowly and smoothly to reduce the size of the initial loop (4), taking great care that this operation does not alter the structure of the knot or the order of the turns. The resulting knot is small and compact and, if properly made, does not damage the main line at all (5). All that remains to be done is to attach the hook (6).

DOUBLE OVERHAND BEND

There are numerous ways of joining two lines of different diameter, some of which are illustrated in the section dealing with bends (see pp. 118–140). Yet, with the exception of the surgeon's knot, these bends are not really suitable for use with gut, as they are often too complex, so we have included an illustration of the double overhand bend which is very quick to make and is very suitable for gut.

Method
This is a simple knot to start; merely place the two lines so that they are parallel but running in opposite directions. Keeping them together, make an overhand knot (1). Add a second turn (2); then tighten the knot by pulling the four ends while pushing the knot from both sides with the fingertips. The finished knot is illustrated in figure 3.

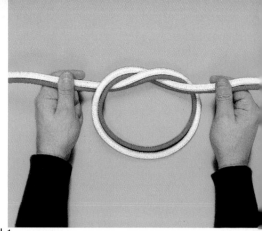
1

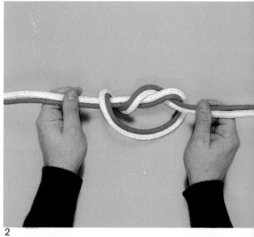
2

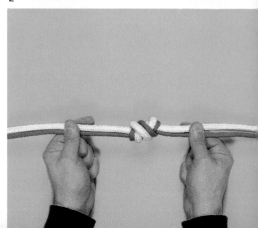

STOPPER KNOT

Quick and easy to make, this stopper knot can also be quite bulky, so it is particularly suited to its purpose.

Method
Using a piece of line of the largest possible diameter, make a loop around the main line (1). Then make a long series of turns to increase both the size of the knot and its grip (2), but check while doing so that they do not overlap or come out of order. Although overlapping turns would certainly enlarge the size of the knot, the advantage would be dubious for it would soon begin to slip. Close the knot by inserting the end into the eye of the loop and tighten it by pulling on the end and the standing part at the same time (3).

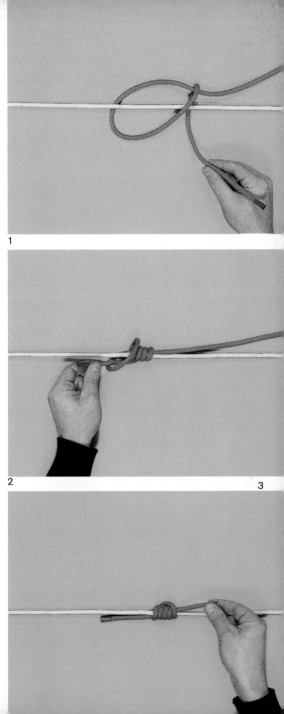

DROPPER LOOP

A loop along a fishing line, known as a dropper loop, can be used in a number of ways and formed by many methods. You can use a second length of gut or, as in this case, make the loop out of the line itself without having to cut it.

There are two big advantages to this loop: it does not slip, and it does not affect the strength of the main line. When it is complete, the line is in perfect alignment and does not seem to be broken up by the loop at all.

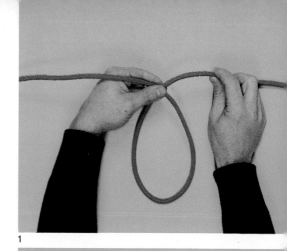

1

2

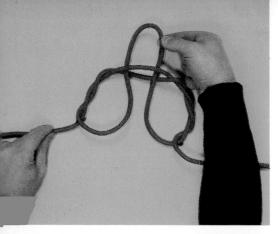

Method

Begin by forming a loop that is a little larger than the actual size you want (1), then using the thumb and index finger twist part of the line around the loop. This creates a series of false turns which would come undone if left to themselves (2). Form a bight in the bottom of the loop (3) and insert it into the central turn (4). Tighten by holding the two ends of the line and pulling the loop (5, 6).

6

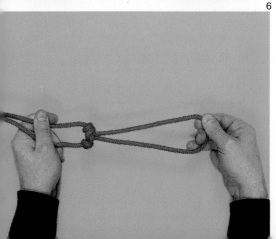

LOOP ON THE BIGHT

This loop, which is a variation on the figure-eight or Flemish loop, owes its popularity to the fact that it is so quick and easy to make. Because it is formed with the line itself it gives maximum guarantee against slip. On the other hand, it has one of the gravest defects a knot can have: it greatly reduces the strength of the line. This fault can be seen clearly in figure 6, where the two ends are shown coming out of the knot parallel. When the line is under tension, the ends are opened out and forced to work against the turn on the far right of the loop. Because of this the knot is not recommended unless you calculate carefully beforehand the strain to which the line will be subjected.

1

2

Method

Begin by making a bight along the line at the point where the loop is required (1). Fold the bight back on itself (2) and make two turns around the standing part (3), taking care to keep the arrangement of the line in perfect order. Pass the bight through the eye on the left and proceed to close the knot (4). Figure 5 shows the knot completed. The size of the loop can be adjusted at this point by pushing the knot to the right or left, making sure that the internal arrangement is not upset. Tighten the knot by pulling the two ends of line and the loop (6).

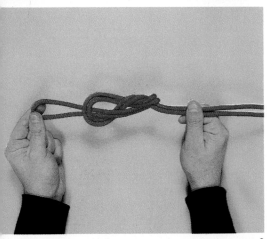

6

SWIVEL HITCHES

First type

There are two rings, one at each end of the swivel, to make it easier to connect the line, so you can use any of the knots described above for hooks with eyes (see pp. 144–157). This particular knot has the added feature that it is a slipped knot, thus allowing the knot to be snugged up to the rings, so that the line becomes one with the swivel.

Method
First pass the end through the ring on the swivel and bring it back around its standing part (1). Then take a number of turns around the bight, tightening them as they are formed (2). Finish the knot by passing the end through the eye of the bight, and tighten the knot by pulling the swivel and the standing part (3).

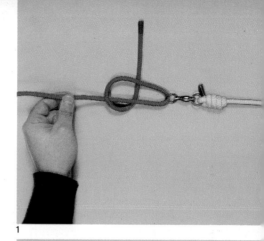

1

2

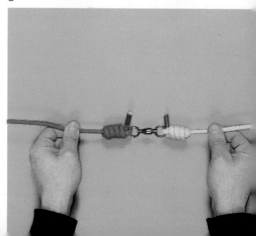

SWIVEL HITCHES

Second type

The double turn through the ring makes this a fixed knot, not a slipped knot. It is easy to make and very strong, even under hard working conditions. The fact that the turns can be doubled or even trebled through the ring gives the knot exceptional resistance to jerks and friction.

Method
Pass the end several times through the ring of the swivel (1). It is not advisable to use too many turns. It is more important to make sure that the turns wind uniformly and in order around the ring. Then make an overhand knot around the standing part (2), taking one or more extra turns to make it more secure (3). Tighten the knot by pulling both the standing part and the swivel.

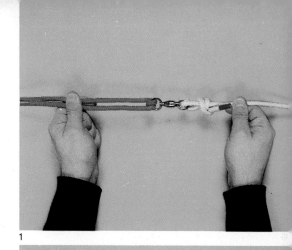

1

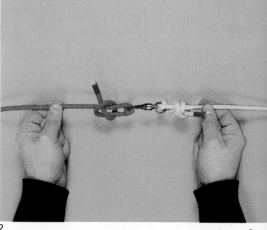

2

3

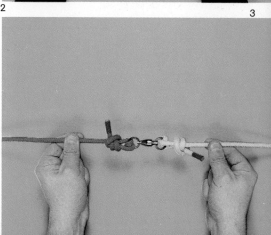

decorative and applied knots

decorative knots

The difference between utility knots and decorative knots is more subtle than it may seem. Generally knots whose only purpose is to decorate or adorn or those made purely for their appearance are classified as decorative. In reality, however, very few knots are purely decorative, for most of them combine aesthetic qualities with specific practical functions which are often quite important.

This chapter does not purport to cover the whole of the enormous field of so-called decorative knots, but the knots presented should at least give some idea of this vast category.

◀ 1. Chain sinnet   2. Monkey's fist
3. Ladder   4. Ocean plat

FOUR-STRAND CROWN SINNET AROUND A CORE

This is an excellent way of covering a cylindrical object and, despite appearances, is not at all complicated to make. The basic weave is identical to that used for the crown sinnet on pages 232–233, the only difference being that in this case the cords are doubled and a cylindrical object is inserted at the beginning. Doubling the cords will cover the core better, but the same result could be obtained by increasing the number of cords to be braided.

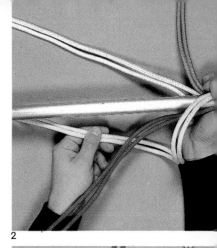

2

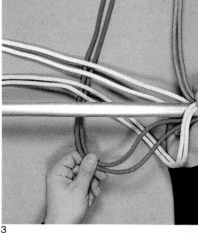

3

1

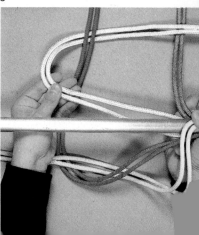

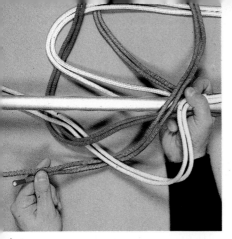

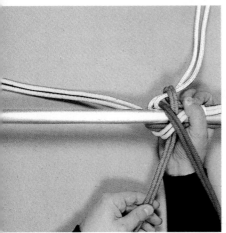

Method

Begin by putting the cords in order (1), as order is an essential part of making the knot, which could otherwise become an inextricable tangle of cord. Form half turns with each pair of cords so that the adjacent pairs can be inserted through them (2, 3, 4). Complete the formation of the half turns (5), then partly tighten them to bring out the typical weave of the crown knot (6).

The pairs of cord in figure 6 are unnaturally arranged towards the right; this has been done purely for the sake of the explanation, but you need only arrange them symmetrically around the metal tube to be able to see the first mesh of the crown sinnet complete. Repeat these steps to form this highly decorative sinnet (7).

7

SIX-STRAND CROWN SINNET AROUND A CORE

Six double cords are used here, as they make it possible to cover even large cylindrical objects. This is not an easy sinnet to make, so it is better to practice first on sinnets that use fewer cords before moving on to this one.

Method
First split the pairs of cord into two groups (1). Pass the bottom pairs (in this case, white, orange, and navy) under the core and interweave them through the top ones, which do not move for the moment (2, 3, 4). Now interweave the upper pairs (tweed, yellow, and blue) through the bottom group, passing them over the core (5, 6, 7). Figure 8 shows the result, with the cords pulled to the right for the sake of clarity. You need only arrange them symmetrically around the tube to see that the first mesh of the sinnet has been successfully completed. Repeat the same steps to produce the completed sinnet (9).

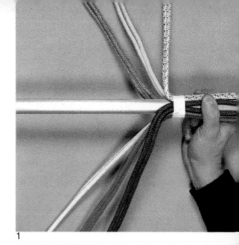

1

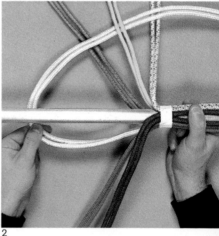

2

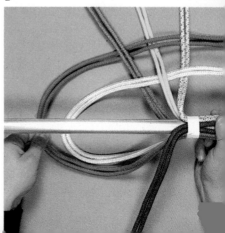

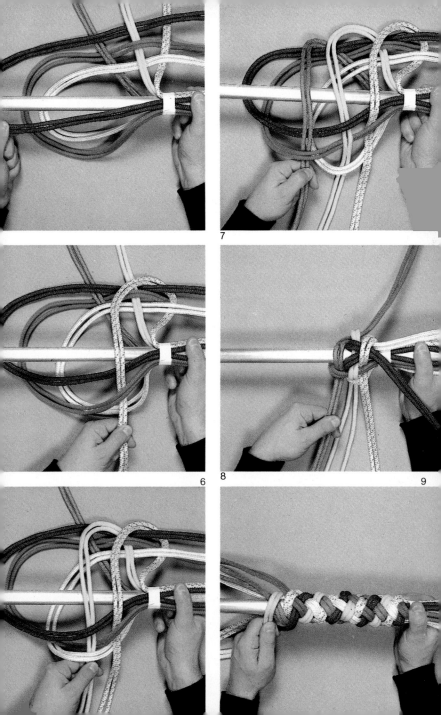

7

6

8

9

WOVEN SINNET

The woven sinnet is a very simple and clever way of covering a cylindrical surface and basically consists of preparing a large number of bights to act as the warp and then weave around them with a weft of one or more cords. This system is open to an infinite number of variations with which you can obtain very good effects.

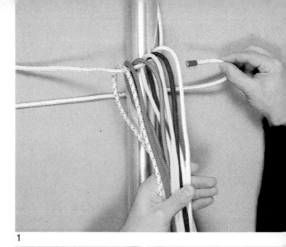

1

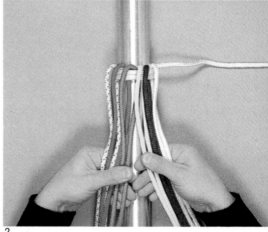

2

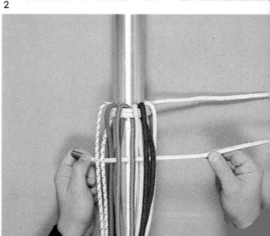

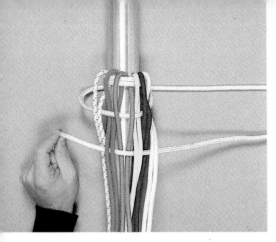

Method

Begin by arranging the bights along the core and fasten them with a couple of turns of the weft cord (1, 2). Continue by interweaving the horizontal cord through the bights (3, 4, 5). We have used a simple two-under-and-two-over weave here, so you really cannot go wrong; but as we have already said, you can use other, more complicated designs requiring more planning and organization. Despite its simplicity, the final result of this pattern is really quite effective (6).

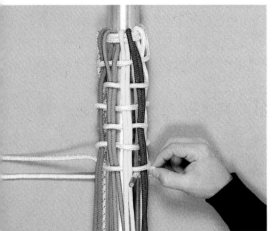

6

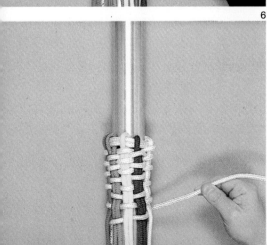

TURK'S HEAD

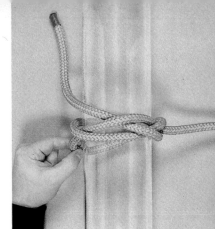

1

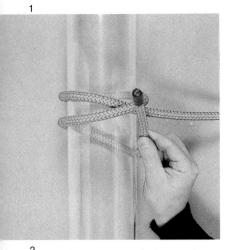

2

3

4

This is a very effective decorative knot that can be tied around cylindrical objects of any size. We have shown the simplest form here, i.e., the one with the least amount of interweaving; but with a little practice you can master the technique and make more complex versions that are even more effective. We have deliberately used a transparent cylinder on which to make the knot so that you can see the weave at the back.

Method
First of all, wind the cord around the cylinder and insert the end under the first turn (1, 2). Note that in the illustrations the end is short only so that you can see where it is in the knot and to avoid the confusion of yards and yards of cord. Cross the turns (3); then weave the end through the bight formed, passing it over the the top cord and under the bottom one. In figure 5 the knot is complete, with the only remaining thing to do being to fill it in and tighten it by doubling it one or more times (6, 7, 8).

MONKEY'S FIST

1

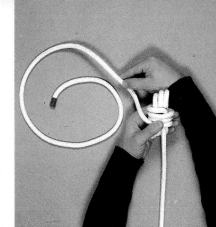

3

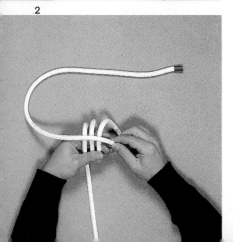

2

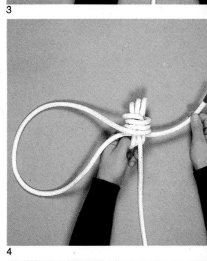

4

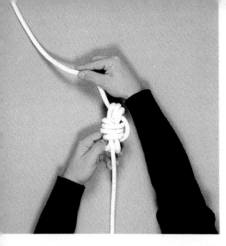

The monkey's fist, also known as the pouch or button, is a typically decorative knot that is also used in many practical ways: it can hold heavy items, such as pieces of lead, inside its turns to give it weight when it is used at the end of a heaving line, and it forms a knob which can substitute for a modern button.

Method
There are no special difficulties in making this knot. Begin by taking three vertical turns (1) around your hand. Hold them with three horizontal turns (2, 3). Now make another three turns around the horizontal turns but inside the vertical turns (4, 5, 6), producing a kind of ball which is round in shape when carefully worked (7, 8).

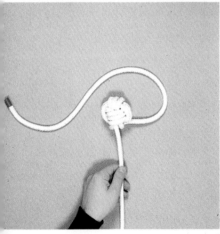

The monkey's fist described above is made by crossing the turns in only three directions: vertical, horizontal, and vertical again. Better, more compact and spherical results can be obtained by increasing the number of turns or the number of times they cross over. A trick to ensure that the ball is round is to make it around a small ball, which then lies hidden inside the knot.

8

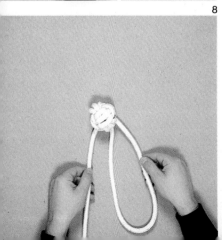

MULTI-STRAND LANYARD KNOTS

First type

Strictly speaking, these knots belong to the category of stopper knots discussed on pages 27–38; but we have decided to include them among the decorative knots, because it is only effectively used as such.

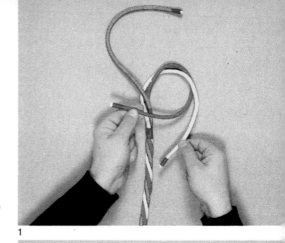

These are only two examples of compound knots. Many weaves (walls, crowns, diamonds, Matthew Walkers) can be used giving very different end results, although they all have the same common feature that they enlarge the rope on which they are made. The number of strands can also vary. This may at first seem a great complication, but you need only practice the knots with three strands, as shown here, to see that when you have mastered the basic technique, more strands do not present insurmountable problems.

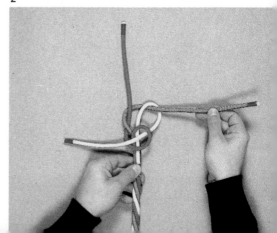

Before moving on to more complicated compound knots, you

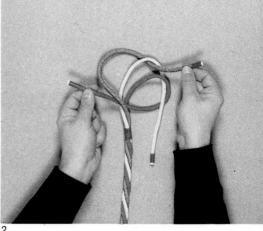

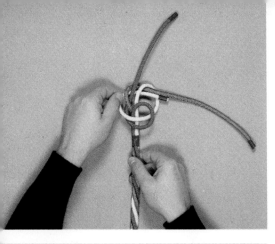

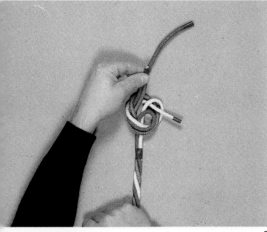

6

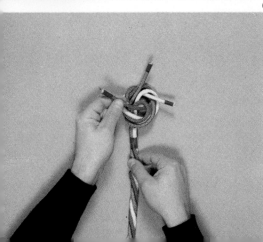

should also practice the diamond knot (see pp. 200–201), the crown (pp. 94–95), and the crown sinnet (see pp. 232–233).

The basic methods are quite similar, and it is precisely for this reason that you should learn to pick out the differences between them. Combining these knots in different ways will allow you to produce imaginative and highly decorative effects, particularly if the knots are made with a good number of strands.

Method
This knot is made in three distinct stages. First, a wall is formed by inserting each strand from below through the bight formed by the one before it (1, 2, 3). In the second stage, the wall is transformed into a full Matthew Walker by bringing the three strands round again from below through the next two bights (4, 5, 6). Figure 7 shows the finished and drawn up crown with the strands all emerging in the same direction. The third stage is to form the crown. There are no particular difficulties in this stage which is clearly shown

195

in figures 8, 9, 10, and
11. Tighten the knot
fully by working the
three strands gradually,
pulling each one in turn
to obtain an almost

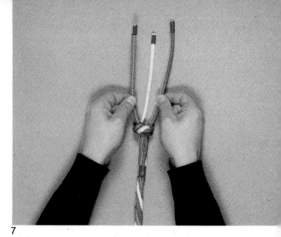

7

8

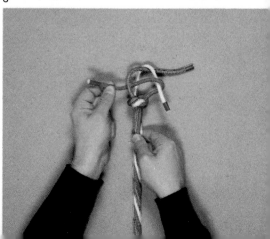

spherical knot with the three ends emerging as in figure 12. To eliminate these, pass them down through the crown.

12

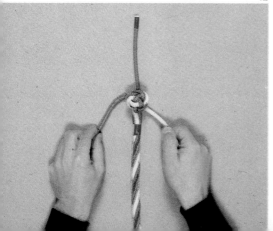

MULTI-STRAND LANYARD KNOTS

Second type

This is an uncomplicated knot which gives an attractive and perfectly round end result.

Method
Begin by inserting each strand through the turn formed by the previous one (1, 2, 3). The weaving in this knot is not exactly straightforward, so study the photographs carefully and follow them exactly. Close the turns into loops (4, 5) to form a structure very similar to the monkey's fist (pp. 192–193) and then to ensure that the knot is round, double the loops by having each strand follow through its own first lead (6, 7, 8). Tighten the knot gradually, pulling each strand a number of times. For a perfectly spherical shape, double the leads again (9).

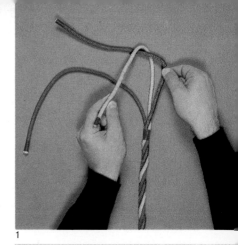

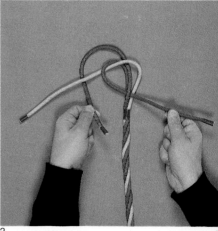

1

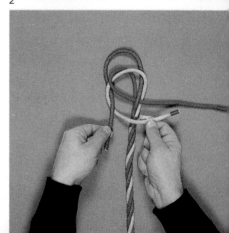

2

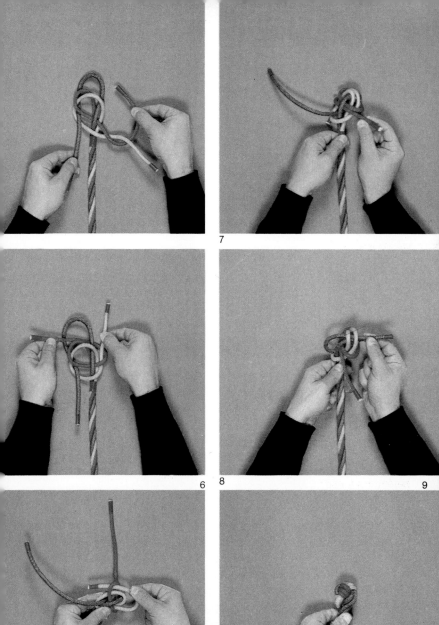

7

6 8 9

TWO-STRAND DIAMOND KNOT

This is a very attractive knot that is excellent for decorating any cord that is to be left in view, such as a knife or whistle lanyard. It may seem difficult at first sight, but provided you have a little patience and do not give up at the first failure, you will be rewarded with very satisfying results.

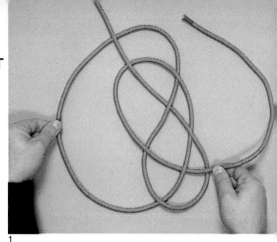

1

2

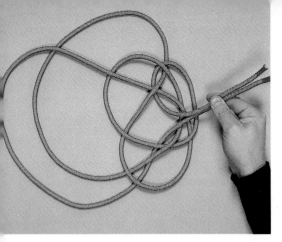

Method

Form a carrick bend (see pp. 136–137) around its own standing part (1). The two free ends follow the two diagonals of the carrick bend, but with the opposite weave (2, 3). All that then remains is to work the knot. To do this, pull the loop left when the carrick bend was formed and the two free ends smoothly and slowly (4, 5). Make sure that there is no overlapping and that the knot tightens evenly and with its internal order intact. Figure 6 shows the knot completed, clearly demonstrating the admirably perfect symmetry from which it probably got its name.

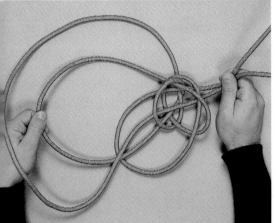

6

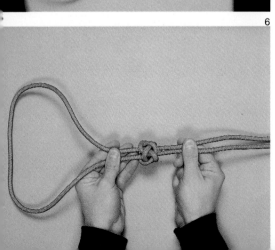

CHINESE BUTTON KNOT

This knot is thousands of years old and is still used today in China and other Eastern countries instead of modern buttons.

Method
The construction of this knot is not simple. It can be made on a support, such as a table, or in the hand. We have chosen the second method because it makes the knot easier to control while it is taking shape. The central shape is the carrick bend (see pp. 136–137), as can be seen in figure 5, which is continued to form four perfectly symmetrical eyes (8). The method for making the knot can be clearly seen in the illustrations. When complete, it should be worked tightly and carefully so that it keeps its symmetrical shape at all times.

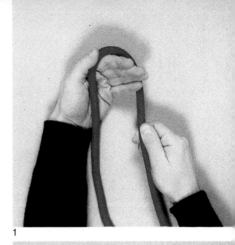

1

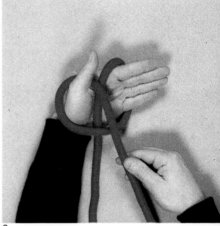

2

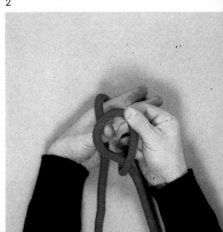

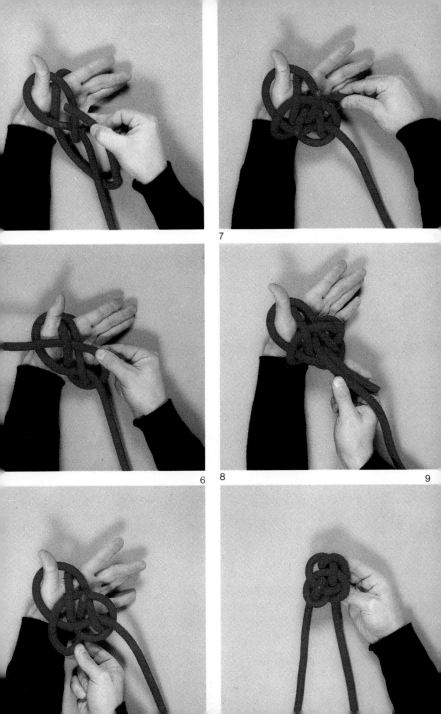

7

6

9

8

CHAIN SINNET

The chain sinnet could not be left out of any manual dedicated to knots. It is very useful for shortening a rope that is too long. It is also quite decorative and makes a very elastic cord.

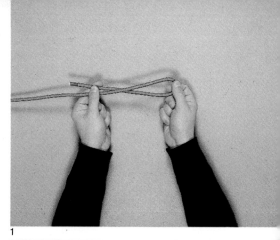

1

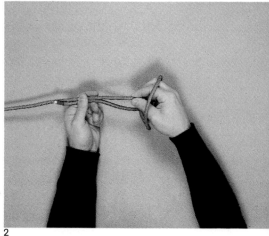

2

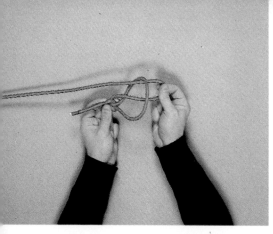

Method

The chain sinnet is very simple to make. It begins with a bight, with the ends held parallel to each other (1). Put your hand through the eye of the bight and take hold of the longer end of the rope (2). Pull your hand out again to form a noose as described on page 101 (3). Now pull a bight from the longer end through the loop of the noose (4). Repeat the operation until the chain reaches the desired length (5, 6).

The chain can be instantly released simply by pulling on the working end. To prevent it undoing, thread the end through the last eye instead of bringing it through in a bight.

6

OCEAN PLAT

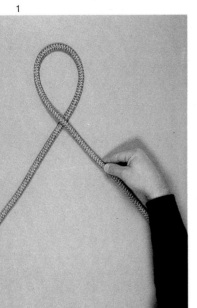

4

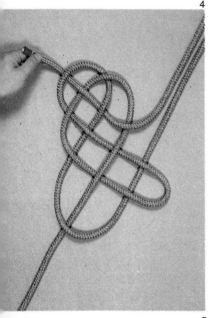

This is a flat knot of a characteristic oval shape. It is highly decorative and finds thousands of applications in all types of situations. It makes a fine door mat, but it can also be used whenever you want to protect an object from wear by rubbing, for example between mooring cables and the sides of a boat. It looks highly complex at first, but if you follow the photo sequence carefully, you will see that it really presents no difficulties at all. The matting illustrated in figure 7, is made with four crossing diagonals. The number of diagonals determines the total size of the mat. Once this number is established, the mat can only be made thicker, not larger. Of course if you increase the number of diagonals, you can make the mat larger, but it is advisable to have a pattern to follow before attempting this variation.

5

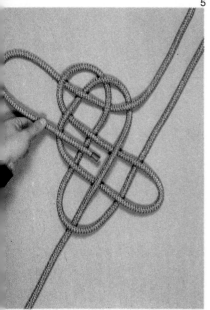

Method
Begin by making a loop at the center of the rope (1). Leaving a bight in the line, make a second loop with the right end, crossing it in the opposite direction (2). Complete one side of the knot by making a bight with the left end (3). Note that so far the rope has not been interwoven at all. Continue working with the left end and begin interweaving the loops that were made previously (4, 5, 6, 7). Take care not to alter

their position when sliding the rope through. You can hold the turns in position by using nails fixed into the board on which you are working, but with a little patience and practice, this will not be necessary. Double the knot by following the arrangement already laid out with one of the ends (8, 9, 10, 11) and follow the same basic principle to double the knot

6

7

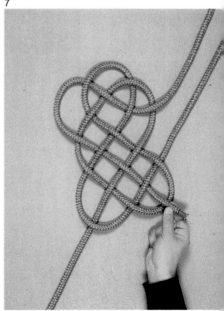

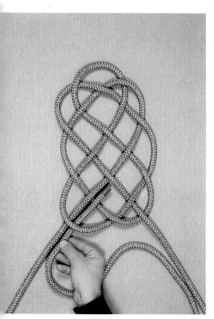

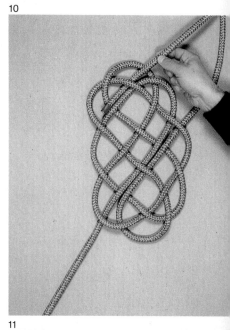

again (12, 13, 14, 15). The only limit to how many times it can be doubled is the physical size of the knot, but increasing the ply of the matting does not increase its size, but only makes it firmer. When it is solid, the matting is finished (16), but there are still a couple more steps to complete to make it more secure, and so ready for use. First of all, pass the ends under the matting and finish them off by tucking them into the weave of the mat, and second, sew up all the points of intersection with a needle and thread.

12

13

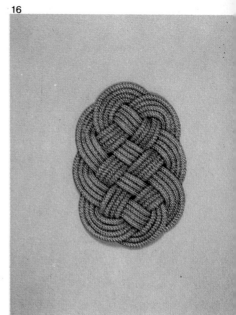

ROUND MATTING

This is a marvellous flat knot which can serve as a mat, a drinks coaster, or as an ornamental knot. The round shape is obtained by making five perfectly symmetrical loops, but even better results are achieved with seven or nine. Before attempting these, however, you should draw out a pattern on a sheet of paper, at least for the initial steps. The method is clearly illustrated in the photographs.

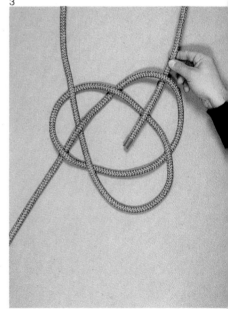

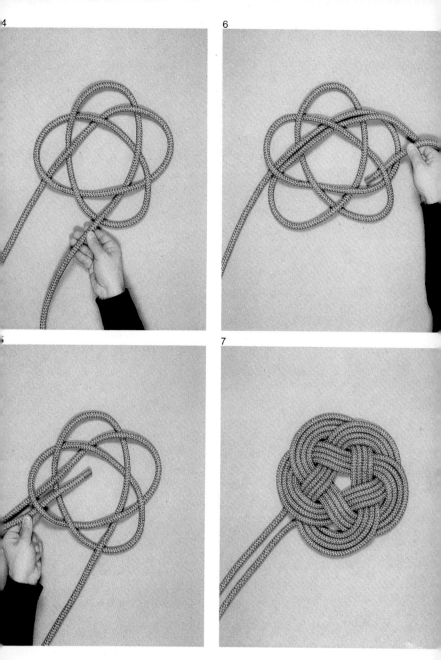

SQUARE MATTING

This matting has a specifically square shape that is obtained by using four intersecting diagonals. A simple variation is to increase the number of interlacing diagonals on the four sides, thus increasing the size of the mat whilst retaining its square shape. Alternatively, you can increase them on one side only to give it a rectangular shape, but it is better to master the technique of making square matting before attempting this. There is nothing particularly difficult about making this mat, and the method is clearly illustrated in the photographs; but a few practical hints may help make the outcome more successful. You need adequate space on which to lay out the matting, as it requires many yards of rope, which are constantly being moved around. Since this can lead to great confusion and make the mat just a mass of tangles, be careful not to move the turns that have already been laid when passing the end through.

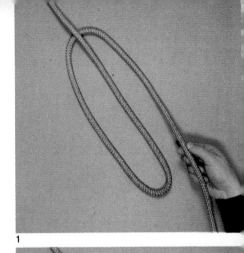

1

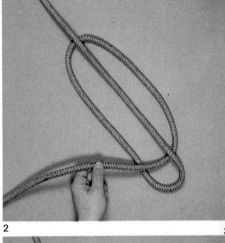

2

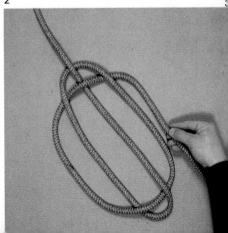

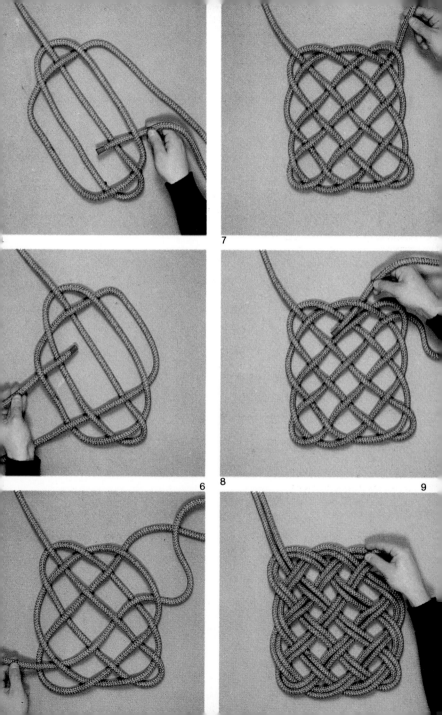

7

6

8

9

FLAT SINNET OR BRAID

Also known as the English, ordinary, or common sinnet, this is the simplest plat, but, nevertheless, it has its own decorative value which makes it suitable for a vast range of applications.

Method
The braid is easily made. All you do is cross the right and left hand cords alternately over the center cord. Figures 1, 2, 3, and 4 show this clearly. Figure 5 is intended only to illustrate the technique, for it shows the plait complete but not tightened, while in reality it is tightened while being made, resulting in a braid like the one shown in figure 6. The plat can be finished off by a number of knots, such as one of the wall and crown combinations (see pp. 194–199).

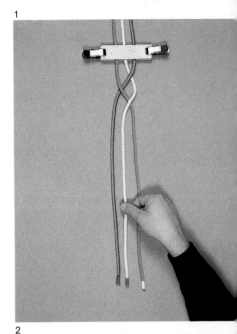

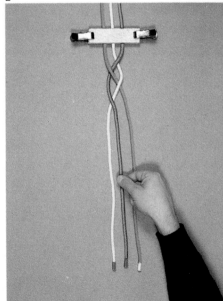

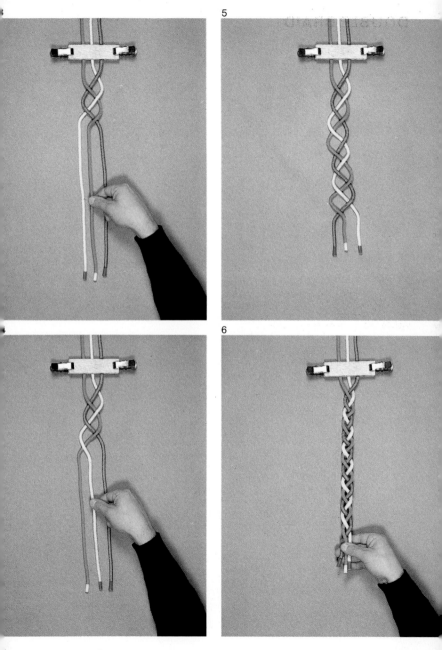

DOUBLE BRAID

Even in its simplicity, the flat sinnet or braid lends itself to a number of interesting variations. This one is obtained merely by doubling the cords and, as you can see, the end result (6) is certainly very decorative.

The method for making this is identical to that used for the previous sinnet, and so needs no further explanation.
Merely follow the illustrations carefully.

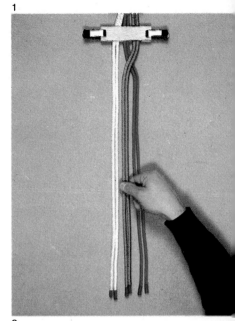

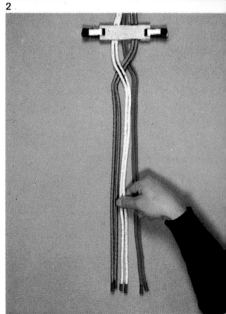

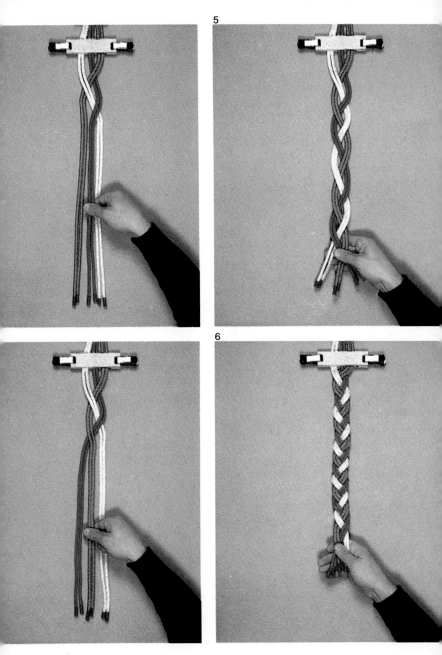

FOUR-STRAND SINNET

First type

Four cords can be used to produce an enormous numbe of plats, all different from each other. The type illustrated on the right, for example, produces a beautiful flat braid, though as you will see further on, square or round cords can also be produced with the same number of strands.

Method
The basic principle is to weave the strand on the right throughout, as shown in figures 1, 2, 3, and 4 which illustrate a complete cycle of the four strands. Figures 5 and 6 show the plat before and after it is tightened.

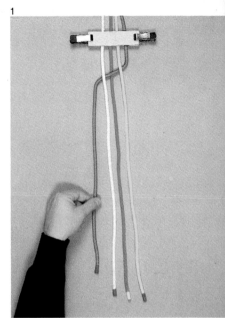

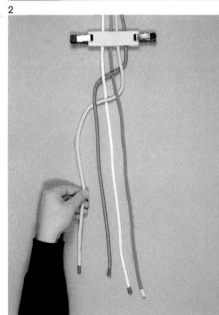

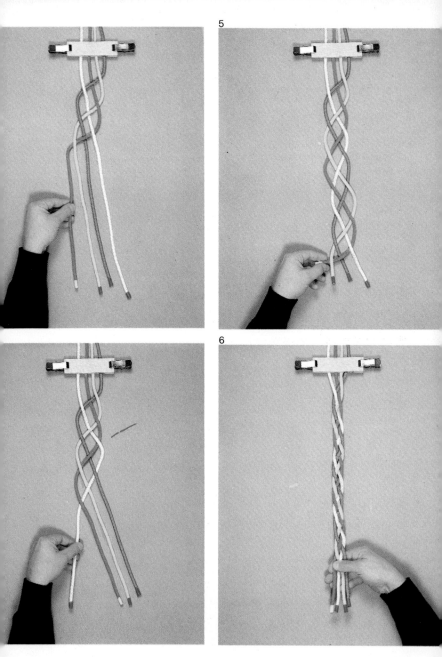

FOUR-STRAND SINNET

Second type

The special feature of this braid is the fact that the two center strands are not braided together, but act as the warp while the two outer ones act as a weft.

Method
Begin by crossing the two outer strands between the two center strands, thus changing their starting positions (1). The cycle is completed by bringing the outer strands back to their original positions after they have been crossed around the center strands (2). Repeat these steps until the braid is completed (3, 4, 5). The end result is a plat that has an almost circular cross section and can be used as a cord (6).

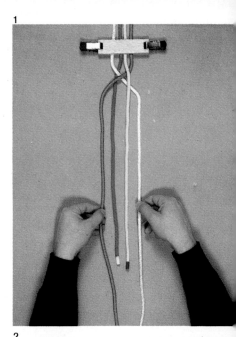

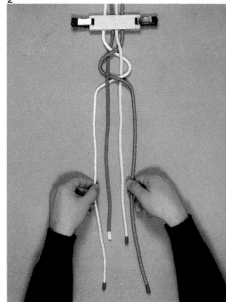

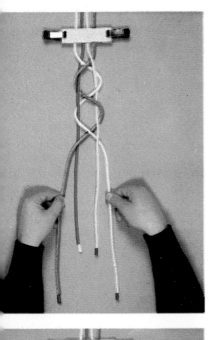

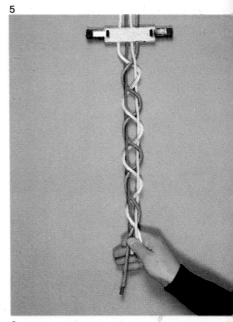

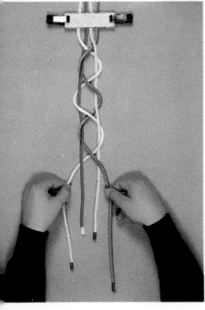

223

FOUR-STRAND SINNET

Third type

This is a marvellous example of a woven plat. As the photos show, three of the strands (in this case white, red, and yellow) make up the warp and one, the blue strand, acts as the weft. The braid should be tightened well each time the blue strand is passed across the others, giving a very ornamental effect which keeps its shape even under great strain. The method is clearly illustrated in the sequence of photographs.

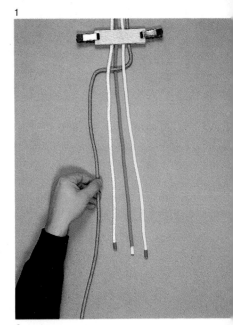

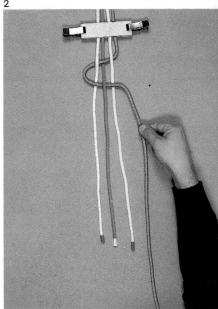

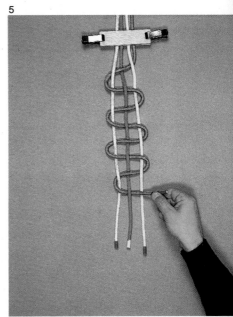

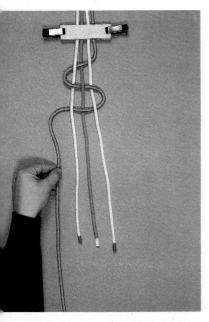

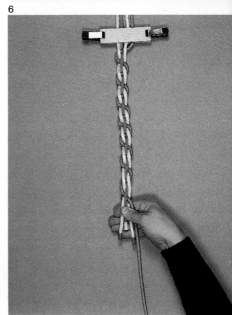

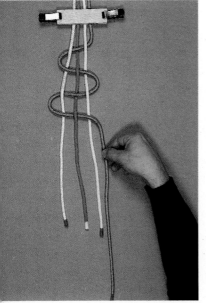

FOUR-STRAND SINNET

Fourth type

This is a little more complicated, but the effectiveness of the result compensates for the patience needed to complete it.

We believe that the best way of making this particular plat is to follow the movements illustrated in the photographs. In doing so, you will see that the basic principle is not really so complex. The braid should be tightened at every step in order to stop it from possible sagging.

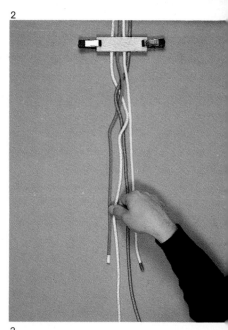

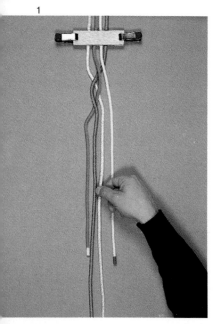

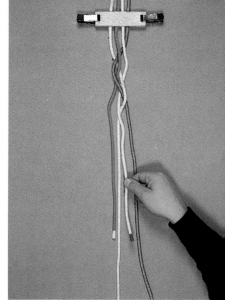

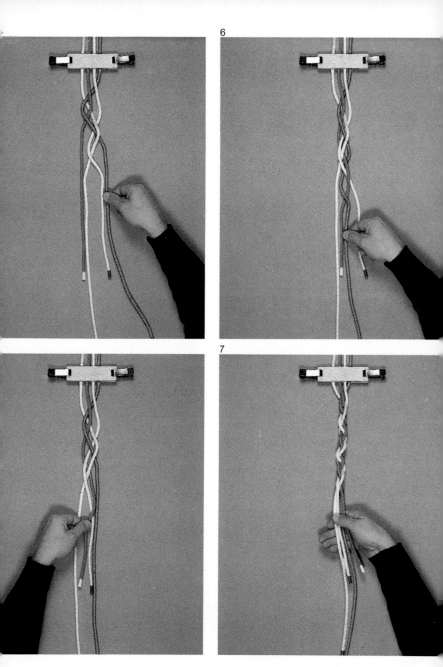

FIVE-STRAND SINNET

This is a very attractive plat that is quite easy to make. Figure 7 clearly shows the end result. The method is easy to understand from the photo sequence; it basically involves bringing the outer strands to the center by crossing them over the two adjacent strands.

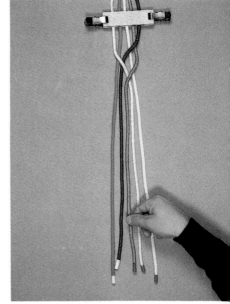

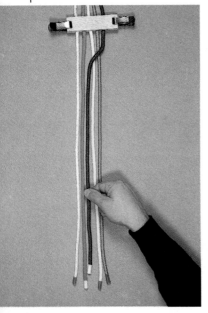

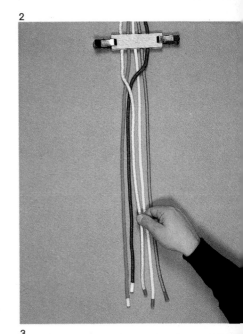

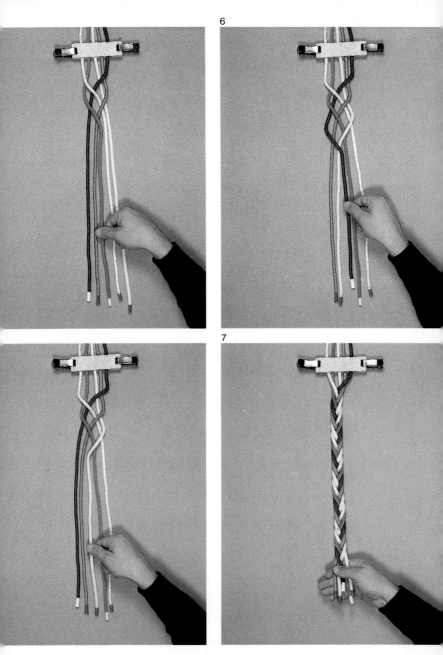

SIX-STRAND SINNET

The number of variations possible with six strands is practically limitless and should satisfy the most imaginative requirements. The braid illustrated here is one of the simplest and only a sample of what can be done. The basic principle of the braid is to bring the right strand over to the left with an over-two-under-one-over-two weave. The maneuvers illustrated in figures 1 and 2 merely provide an attractive beginning for the sinnet and are not repeated.

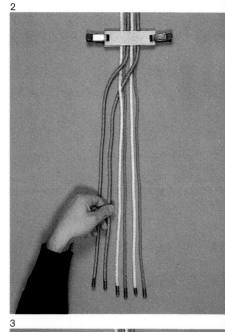

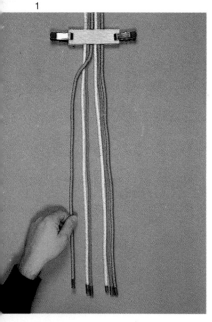

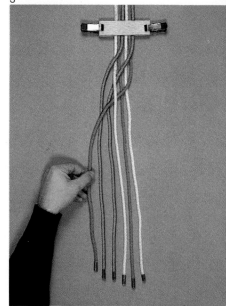

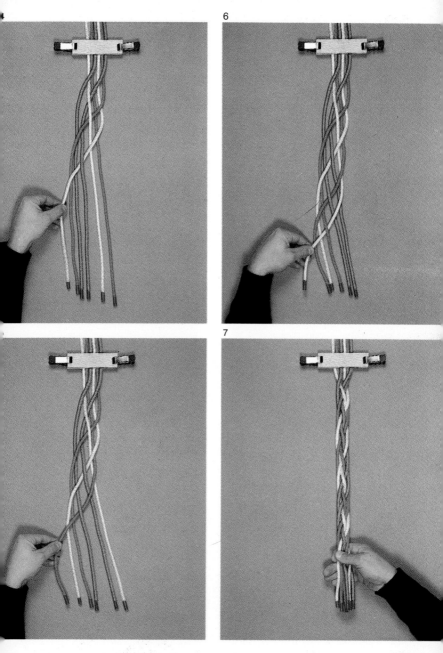

CROWN SINNET

The crown sinnet can be made with a variable number of strands producing different weaves that can be used as cords or coverings. Figure 5 shows that any cylindrical object could be inserted in the center and would be completely covered by the sinnet. The use of this sinnet as a covering is discussed in more detail on pages 184–185.

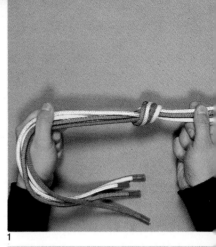

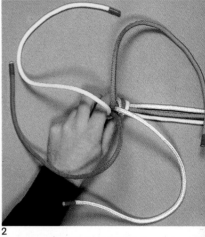

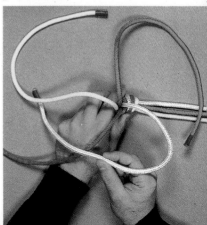

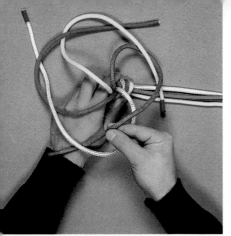

Method

This sinnet is very easy to make. Begin with an overhand bend made with all four strands (1). Figures 2 and 3 show the preparation for the basic crowning shown in figure 4. Working always in one direction (in this case clockwise), insert each strand in the turn formed by the subsequent strand. This produces a closed shape which is the basis of the crown sinnet. Figure 5 shows the knot being tightened and demonstrates how a cylindrical object could be inserted as described above. Finally, figure 6 shows the finished sinnet and how decorative it is. It can be finished off by tucking the four strands into the center.

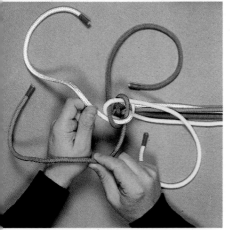

6

FIGURE-EIGHT CHAIN

The figure-eight knot (see pp. 31–35) finds yet another of its many uses in this pretty chain. It can be used as a belt or strap for a shoulder bag, or for shortening and decorating any cord that is going to be on view.

The method is very simple and clearly shown in the illustrations: simply make a series of figure-eight knots all in the same direction. Be sure to tighten them well to avoid any unwanted sagging when the chain is under strain.

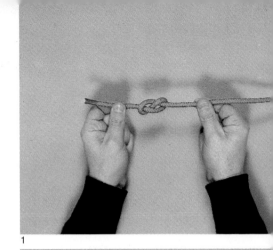

1

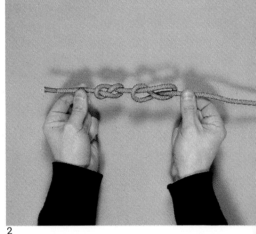

2

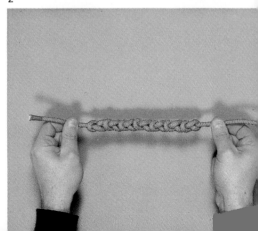

applied knots

Knots can be used together in an infinite number of combinations, each time with different and often surprising results, and we thought it would be useful to group in this chapter some of those combinations which are worthy of mention because of their particular usefulness or originality. They include simple applications like the net and more complicated ones such as the ladder: just a few examples of what can be done with a simple piece of rope.

With a little patience and imagination, you can create truly ingenious results, possibly with a spark of genius.

LADDER

Begin by forming a figure-eight knot (see pp. 31–35) in the bight of the rope; then separate the ends and lay them parallel to determine the width of the rungs. With the left end make a double bight around the right end (1). Using the right end, make a series of turns around the bight, tightening each one immediately (3, 4, 5). Finish the rung by passing the end through the loop at the end of the bight (6, 7). Note that this rung is simply a running knot secured on both sides, so, before passing on to the next rung, make sure that the turns are well tightened (8). This will balance the rung and avoid subsequent sagging. Once the rung is tight, you can continue using the same procedure, working from the right alternately, to make the required number of rungs (9).

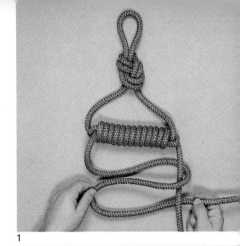

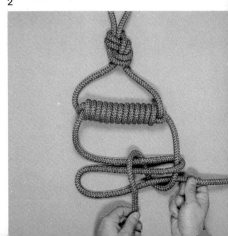

236

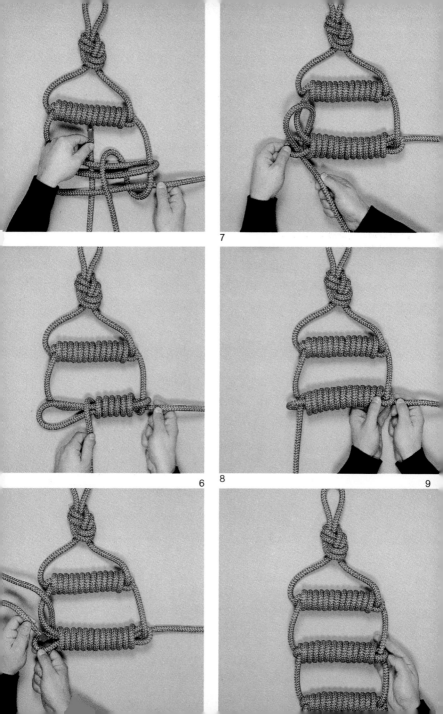

NETTING

The mesh of a net,
whether destined for
fishing or to make a bag
or a hammock, can be
made with various
types of knot. The
choice depends on the
use to which the net is
going to be put and the
degree of elasticity that
will be required. Three
useful mesh knots are
illustrated on page 239:
The sheet bend (figure
4 and pp. 122–125)
makes a net that is not
very elastic and does
not lose shape easily.
The reef knot (figure 5
and pp. 128–129) gives
the net a certain degree
of elasticity but has very
little resistance to
deformation. Finally,
the carrick bend (figure
6 and pp. 136–137)
produces a very firm
and practically
undeformable knot.

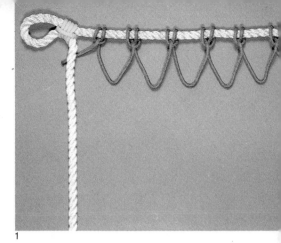

1

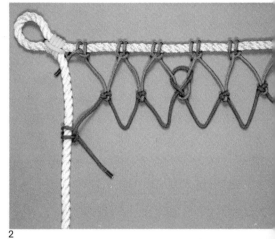

2

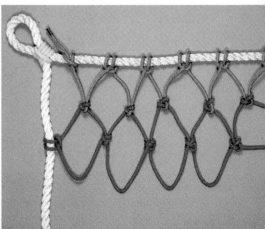

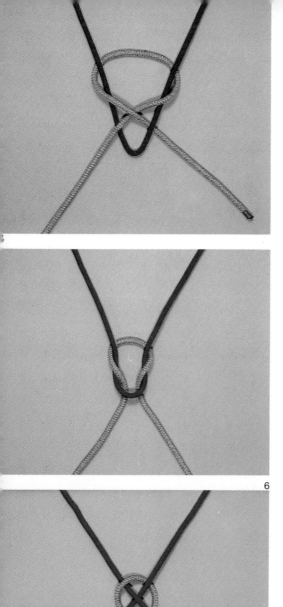

When making the net, the starting point is the headline, the frame rope, which has to take all the strain from the mesh. It has to be very thick and strong compared to the rope used for the net. The mesh can be connected to the frame rope by clove hitches (see pp. 42–54) or cow hitches (p. 57).

6

STAGE OR SCAFFOLD HITCH

The boatswain's chair at sea and the swing on land are both planks suspended from two ropes to form hanging chairs. Whether used to support a man at the top of a yard or to amuse a child, its purpose is always to support a person in mid-air, and so the ropes have to be tied very carefully. A sure and simple way of doing this is by preparing a plank with two small battens at right angles to it at each end.

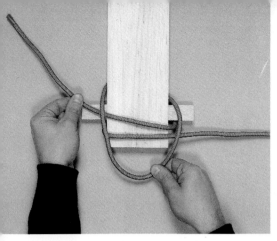

Method
Take a rope around the plank and batten as illustrated in figures 1, 2, and 3; then pull the innermost turn over the end of the plank (4) to give a completely secure grip (5). Finish it off with a bowline (see pp. 70–85) (6), but before tightening the knot, check that the support rope on both sides is perfectly perpendicular to the plank.

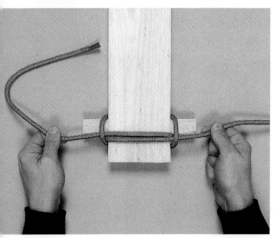

6

GUIDE KNOT

This is actually a figure-eight knot (see pp. 31–35) formed in the bight of a rope, but we have included it here, because it is so popular with mountain guides. Other safety knots that can be used in mountaineering can be found in the sections dealing with loops (pp. 67–98) and hitches (pp. 39–66).

Method
Middle the rope (1), and, allowing a long enough bight for the loop desired, twist the rope with the right hand, taking care not to alter the parallel arrangement of the rope (2, 3). Pass the bight (4) through the eye of the twist (5) to produce a perfectly balanced and ordered figure-eight knot. Check the knot, adjust the loop to fit around the waist, and tighten (6).

3

5

4

6

243

SAFETY HARNESS

The sequence of photographs shows an ingenious safety harness that can be used for climbing or sailing whenever a custom-made harness is not available. It is extremely safe as regards grip, but the same cannot be said for speed with which it can be released. The only solution is to cut the rope with a knife which you should always keep handy whenever you are exposed to risks and danger. The harness can be made by following the illustrations carefully.

2

1

3

GLOSSARY

bend, to: to tie two ropes together by their ends.

bight: the loop or slack part formed when a rope is doubled back upon itself.

bitts: wooden uprights, usually in pairs, on the deck of a ship, used to secure large ropes or hawsers.

block: in sailing, this refers to a pulley with one or more sheaves in a single frame.

bollard: a post, usually round and made of metal, on the deck of a ship or a warf, used for tying up or mooring.

capsize, to: said of a knot when it changes shape or deforms under stress so that it loosens or slips.

clear, to: to free rigging from any obstacles; to loosen tangles in a rope.

cleat: a metal or wooden object with two horns around which rope is belayed.

clockwise: the direction of rotation of the hands of a clock.

close hauled: the trim of the sail when sailing as close to the wind as practical.

cordage: rope in general; in sailing, it includes wire rope.

core: the heart or inner part of a rope or sinnet.

counterclockwise: the direction opposite to the rotation of the hands of a clock.

downhaul: a rope or tackle used for hauling down a sail.

earings: small ropes in the corners of sails used for reefing.

ease off, to: to slacken or let out a rope.

end: as opposed to the standing part, the part of the rope with which the knot is tied.

eye of a rope: a loop formed at the end of a rope by splicing or seizing.

fairleader: a wooden, plastic, or metal piece with holes, used to direct running rigging; it is lashed into the ship's rigging.

fall: the part of a tackle which passes through the blocks and to which the strain is applied.

fender: a cushion of elastic material to protect the sides of a boat from knocks. Grommet rings may be used as fenders.

fid: a conical wooden tool used to work or undo knots and lines.

flake: a turn or turns in a coil of rope.

footrope: a rope fixed beneath the yards of sailing ships, supported by brackets and used by sailors when maneuvering the sails.

foul, to: said of a rope when it cannot slide because it is jammed or tangled.

fray, to: to unravel, especially the end of a rope.

grommet or grommet ring: a wire or rope ring made from a single line wrapped around itself so it won't slip. It is often used to hold tackle blocks.

halyard: rope for hoisting sails or yards.

handrail: rope or metal rail at the sides of steps for support.

haul, to: to pull a rope or tackle by hand.

haul taut, to: to pull or stretch a rope to the limit.

hawser: plain-laid or hawser-laid (left-handed) rope large enough for mooring or towing. It is usually five to twenty-four inches around.

heaving line: a light line attached to the mooring line with a weighted knot at the end. It is tossed onto the wharf and used to haul the larger line ashore.

hoist, to: in sailors' language, to lift weights, sails, flags, etc. with running rigging.

lanyard: thin three-strand or braided cotton rope, usually used as a handle for tools and gear or to make fast rigging.

lash, to: in sailors' language, to tie down moveable objects on board.

lashing: generally any rope or small stuff used to lash objects.

lay: the twisting of the strands forming a rope.

lay hold, to: in seamanship, to grasp or put strain on a rope.

laying up: the right handed or left handed twisting in making a rope.

leads: parts of a tackle between the blocks.

let go by the run, to: (also, to let run) to let go of a rope or rigging suddenly.

lift: hawser or tackle from mast to boom which holds the weight of the latter, allowing it to be topped at the desired angle.

line: a general term for all rope at sea.

marline: heavy string or twine made up of two or three strands.

marlingspike or marline spike: a pointed metal tool (spike) used for untying reluctant knots or unlaying a rope.

pay out, to: to slack away slowly, strike, or let slip.

pendant: (also, hanger) short length of rope with an eye spliced in one end and a hook in the other.

plain-laid rope: three-stranded rope twisted (laid) to the right.

point: the conical decorative end of a rope or other line used to help reeve it through holes and eyes.

rails and stanchions: the safety rail along a deck.

reef points: short lengths of rope which hang down on either side of a sail by means of which the sail can be tied down (reefed).

rigging: all the rope and line on a sailing ship. There is a distinction between the standing rigging (shrouds and stays, which are fixed) and the running rigging (sheets, halyards, etc., which are tied down at one end only).

rope: any cord measuring over one inch around.

running: in seamen's language, this refers to the moving rigging as opposed to the standing rigging.

sheet: running rigging used to control the lower corner of a sail to keep it at the proper tension against the wind.

shroud: standing rigging for lateral support of the mast.

slack: the part of the rope not under tension or running free.

small stuff: twine, cord, etc. Any rope under an inch in circumference.

standing: in seamen's language, it refers to the fixed rigging as opposed to the running rigging. In a rope the standing part is the part which is fixed or under tension as opposed to the end which is free and with which the knot is tied.

stay: standing rigging which supports the mast longitudinally.

stopper: a short length of rope or chain used to limit the running of a line or to hold lines firmly while they are being cleated. One end of the stopper is attached to the ship; the other end is tied around the line to be stopped.

strand: twisted yarns which are joined together to form a rope.

stretching: tension applied to new rope before it is used.

strike, to: to lower a sail or a flag.

tack: the forward corner of a sail. Also the direction of the bow of a boat with relation to the wind. If the wind is coming over its right side, the boat is said to be on a starboard tack; if it is coming over the left side, the boat is tacking to port.

turn: one round of a rope, it is the basic element of the knot. To take a turn is to make a single round with the rope around a cleat or bollard, etc.

warp: to shift a vessel from one place to another in a harbor by means of ropes.

whipping: protection given to a rope by winding string or small stuff around it to prevent it from wearing or fraying.

work, to: to draw up and shape a knot.

yarn: the basic element in the construction of a rope, it is made up of twisted fibers.

KNOTS AND THEIR USE

As the reader will have seen in the previous pages, most (though not all) of the knots in this guide bear the stamp of the sea; and this, in fact, corresponds to the history of this particular branch of human invention. Yet this does not mean that if you know the characteristics of a good sailor's knot, you cannot use it in other areas such as climbing or camping. The following summaries may therefore be useful. The knots discussed in this book are listed under the four main categories in which they are most used: climbing, camping, sailing, and fishing, giving for each activity a set of knots that would be useful to know.

Climbing knots

Cow hitch	page 57
Safety harness	,, 244–245
Bowline	,, 78–79
Rolling hitch	,, 62–63
Heaving line knot	,, 36–37
Guide knot	,, 242–243
Reef knot	,, 127–129
Figure-eight knot	,, 30–35
Carrick bend	,, 136–137
Simple tackle	,, 116
Clove hitch made on a ring	,, 44–45
Double clove hitch	,, 42–43, 54
Ladder	,, 236–237

Camping knots

Cow hitch	,, 57
Angler's loop	,, 96–97
Bowline	,, 70–81
Running bowline	,, 102–103
Knotted sheepshank	,, 114
Artillery loop	,, 98
Sheet bend	,, 122–126
Multiple overhand knot	,, 38
Highwayman's hitch	,, 64–65
Heaving line knot	,, 36–37
Tarbuck knot	,, 106
Bill hitch	,, 55
Hunter's knot	,, 131

Water knot ,, 138–139
Reef knot ,, 127–129
Constrictor knot ,, 66
Noose ,, 101
Overhand knot ,, 28–29
Carrick bend ,, 136–137
Matting ,, 206–215
Simple and complex tackle ,, 116–117
Single and double clove hitch on a post ,, 42–43
Ladder ,, 236–237

Sailing knots

Stage or scaffold hitch ,, 240–241
Cow hitch ,, 57
Safety harness ,, 244–245
Bowline on a bight ,, 84–85
Portuguese bowline ,, 82–83
Bowline ,, 76–77, 80–81
Spanish bowline ,, 86–89
Jury mast knot ,, 90–91
Half hitches ,, 58–59
Fisherman's bend ,, 60–61
Sheet bend ,, 122–126
Rolling hitch ,, 62–63
Heaving line knot ,, 36–37
Sheepshank ,, 110–113
Reef knot ,, 127–129
Figure-eight knot ,, 30–35
Matting ,, 206–213
Poldo tackle ,, 118
Simple and complex tackle ,, 116–117
Single and double clove hitch on a post ,, 42–43
Multi-strand lanyard knots ,, 194–199
Monkey's fist ,, 192–193
Ladder ,, 236–237
Sinnets ,, 184–191

Fishing knots

Loop on the bight ,, 176–177
Dropper Loop ,, 174–175
Angler's Loop ,, 96–97
Knots for eye hooks ,, 145–157
Knots for flatted hooks ,, 158–167
Stopper knot ,, 173
Branch or dropper knot ,, 170–171
Swivel hitches ,, 178–179
Double overhand bend ,, 172
Water knot ,, 138–139
Double fisherman's knot ,, 140–141
Barrel knot ,, 168–169
Netting ,, 238–239

BIBLIOGRAPHY

Ashley, C. W. *The Ashley Book of Knots*, Garden City, New York, 1944.
Berthier, M. P. G. *The Art of Knots*, Garden City, New York, 1977.
Blandford, P. W. *Practical Knots and Ropework*, Blue Ridge Summit, Pennsylvania, 1980.
Brown, T. and R. Hunter. *The Spur Book of Knots*, Bucks, 1978.
Burgess, J. T. *Knots, Ties and Splices*, London, 1977.
Fry, E. C. *Knots and Ropework*, New York, 1977.
Gibson, W. B. *Fells Official Guide to Knots and How to Tie Them*, New York, 1961.
Grainger, S. E. *Creative Ropecraft*, New York, 1977.
Graumont, R. *Handbook of Knots*, London, 1977.
Jarman, C. and B. Beavis. *Modern Rope Seamanship*, Camden, Maine, 1976.
Kreh, L. and M. Sosin. *Practical Fishing and Boating Knots*, London, 1975.
Portalupi, R. *Il libro della pesca in acque dolci*, Milan, 1976.
Snyder, P. and A. Snyder. *Knots and Lines*, Tuckahoe, New York, 1970.

INDEX

anchor bend, 61
angler's knot, 138
angler's loop, 67, 69, 96–97
applied knots, 235–245
  see also decorative knots
artillery loop, 67, 98

barrel knot, 168–169
bends, 119–141, 172
bill hitch, 39, 55
blood knot, 38, 168
boatsman's knot, 42
boatswain's chair, 240
bowline, 8, 67–68, 70–89, 118
  casting, 72–73
  climber's, 78–79
  loop method, 70–71
  on a bight, 67–68, 84–85
  one-handed, 76–77
  Portuguese, 67–68, 82–83
  running, 99, 100–101,
    102–103
  slipped, 71
  Spanish, 67–68, 86–89
  two-fingered, 74–75
  under tension, 80–81
braid, 216–217
  double, 218–219
branch, 170–171
Bulin knot, 70
button, 193

cable
  coiling down, 18
  hanging, 20–21
  storing, 22–23
  tackle, 101
carrick bend, 119, 121, 132,
    136–137, 201, 202, 238
cat's paw hitch, 39, 40, 56
chair knot, 86

Chinese button knot, 202–203
cleat, 247
  using, 19
clove hitch, 8, 39, 42–54, 238
  around post, 42
  double, 42–43, 54
  figure eight, 48–49
  half hitches, 39, 41, 46–47
  looped, 48–49
  on ring, 39, 41, 44–45
  slipped, 42–43
  triple, 54
  two hands, 50–51
  under strain, 52–53
complex tackle, 116–117
constrictor knot, 39, 41, 66
cordage, 9–17, 247
  maintenance, 16
  materials, 11
  structure, 9–11
  see also fibers
cotton, 9, 12
cowboy knot, 136
cow hitch, 39, 41, 57, 238
cross knot, 93
crossing knots, 39

decorative knots, 27, 181–234,
    235–245
diamond knot, 194, 195
  two-strand, 200–201
draw hitch, 64–65
dropper knotting, 170–171
dropper loop, 174–175

English knot, 138
Englishman's knot, 138
eye hooks, knots for, 145–157,
    178

fibers, 9, 11–16

aramid, 12, 13–14, 15
natural, 12 *see also* cotton,
    hemp, manilla
polyamide, 12, 13, 14, 15
polyester, 11, 12, 13, 14, 15
polyethylene, 12, 13, 14
polypropylene, 12, 14, 15
synthetic, 9, 12–16
figure-eight chain, 234
figure-eight knot, 8, 26–27,
    30–32, 141, 234, 236, 242
    in series, 34–35
    slipped, 33
fisherman, knots for, 138,
    143–179
fisherman's bend, 39, 41, 58,
    60–61, 162–163
fisherman's knot, 138
    double, 140–142
flag bend, 122
flattened hooks, knots for,
    158–167
Flemish loop, 176
Franciscan knot, 36

grapevine knot, 119, 121,
    140–141
guide knot, 242–243
gun tackle, 115

half hitch, 39, 41, 46–47, 58,
    110–111, 112
    slipped, 59
hangedman's knot, 104
hangman's knot, 99, 100–101,
    104–105
heaving line knot, 26–27, 36–37,
    160–161
hemp, 9, 12
highwayman's hitch, 39–40,
    64–65
hitches, 39–66, 242
Hunter's bend, 119, 121, 131

Japanese bend, 119–120,
    134–135
jury mast knot, 67, 69, 90–91, 93

ladder, 182–183, 236–237
lanyard hitch, 57
lanyard knots, 194–199
laying up, 9, 248

multi-strand, 198–199
loops, 67–98, 242
loop knot, 107–108, 109
loop on the bight, 176–177
lovers' knot, 27, 30
luff tackle, 115

Magnus/Manger's hitch, 62
manilla, 9, 12
masthead knot, 90
Matthew Walker weave, 194,
    195
matting, 207–215
    round, 212–213
    square, 214–215
mesh knots, 238–239
monkey's fist, 182–183,
    192–193, 198
monk's knot, 36

netting, 238–239
noose, 99, 100–101
nylon *see* fibers, polyamide

ocean plat, 182–183, 206–211
olefin *see* fibers, polypropylene
overhand knot, 26–27, 28–29,
    66, 93, 114, 131, 139, 179
    double, 172
    loops, 136
    multiple knot, 26–27, 38,
    158–159

peg knot, 42
Poldo tackle, 118
Portuguese bowline, 67, 82–83
pouch, 193
Prusik knot, 62

reef knot, 119, 121, 126,
    128–129, 132, 136, 238
    capsizing, 130
    slipped, 129
rolling hitch, 39, 40, 62–63
    slipped, 63
rope *see* cordage
runner tackle, 115
running knots, 99–106

safety harness, 244–245
Savoy knot, 30
scaffold hitch, 240–241

sheepshank, 107–108, 110–113
  knotted, 107–108, 114
sheet bend, 8, 119, 120,
    122–123, 124–125
  double, 123
  left-hand, 126
  slipped, 123
  triple, 123
shortenings, 107–114
simple tackle, 116–117
single bow, 129
single hitch, 58
sinnet
  common, 216
  chain, 182–183, 204–205
  crown, 184–187, 195,
    228–231, 232–233
  English, 216
  five-strand, 228–229
  flat, 216–219
  four-strand, 220–227
  four-strand crown, 184–185,
    195
  ordinary, 216
  six-strand, 230–231
  six-strand crown, 186–187
  woven, 188–189
sisal, 9, 12

slip knots, 99
Spanish burton, 117
split knot, 136
square knot, 119, 122, 128–129,
    134
stage hitch, 240–241
stopper knots, 26–38, 173, 194
surgeon's knot (bend), 119, 121,
    132–133
suture knot, 132
swivel hitch, 178–179

tackle, 115–118
Tarbuck knot, 99, 100–101, 106
thief knot, 127
three-part crown knot, 67, 69,
    94–95, 194, 195
true-lover's knot, 67, 92–93, 138
Turk's head, 190–191

utility knots, 25–141, 183

wall weave, 194
warp knot, 136
water knot, 119–120, 138–139
weaver's knot, 119, 124
winding tackle, 115